Magick

Kitchen

A real-world spiritual guide for manifesting the Kitchen Witch within.

By Leandra Witchwood

Dedication

I dedicate this book to my mother. She was a woman of strength and joy. Through food and laughter, she knew how to connect with others. Her life was not an easy one, and yet she managed to live it with joy and amazing food.

I dedicate this book to my friends and family (especially my husband and kids)! Thank you for enduring all the taste tests, giving me space to write, the runs to the grocery store, the quirky recipes and believing in my abilities.

I also dedicate this book to Witches everywhere. We are a unique breed, full of endless possibilities, competence, beauty, and love. Your gifts are valuable, and I hope you use them well.

Table of Contents

Introduction

Merry Meet and Welcome!

I want to tell you a quick story about a Witch. She was a Kitchen Witch, one who was able to make joyful Magick in the kitchen, with little to no effort. This woman was a single Mother of 3, who had no choice but to be self-sufficient. She got pregnant at 16, during a time when you were expected to marry the father, and submit to what was considered "traditional family values." Years later when her third child was about a year old, her husband left her for another woman. She was scared, alone and broken with three mouths to feed and no help in sight.

However, she had skills. She could remain joyful when she wanted to break down and cry. She was also able to cook a meal fit for royalty, using meager ingredients. "A Champagne taste, on a beer budget" as she would often say. Her skills surpassed anyone I have ever known, in flavor and efficiency. There was no doubt about her resourcefulness and tenacity. She had no official training, but she could learn a new cooking technique or skill instantly. She only needed to be shown once. Her skills in the kitchen ranged from canning and preserving to lavish Thanksgiving dinners where the turkey sat in a brine for three days, complete with from scratch cranberry sauce; to your basic weeknight-slow cooker family style meals.

Here is the thing, I don't think she ever knew what a Kitchen Witch was. She certainly did not identify herself as one. She just had a natural talent in the kitchen to make food Magickal. The energy she raised was subtle and personal. The love for her family and her love for cooking would shine through in every bite. The aromas from her kitchen were spellbinding, leaving no one able to resist her Seared Steak or Chicken Adobo with Rice.

She learned to cook foods from all over the world, from other cooks she befriended. A person's skin color or country of origin did not matter to this pioneer of a woman. She was a master at making the good old American Pot Roast dinner, with garlic mashed potatoes and perfect gravy. She was a magician at Pilipino cuisine, Chinese, Mexican, and more. She cooked with a variety of ingredients from candied rose petals to sinfully dark chocolate.

While she cooked, she gave you her all. She filled her dishes with joy and was always willing to teach. I remember climbing up on chairs to help her retrieve ingredients. I would help her measure and stir. She would hand me her favorite wooden spoon, which was far too large for my little hands; as she would show me her techniques.

This woman was very unassuming. She was well dressed and made up, despite not being wealthy or holding a prestigious career. She had charm and a beautiful smile. She struggled through life more than most, but in the kitchen, she shined. In the kitchen, she was a Queen. The Queen of flavor, texture, and aroma. She never measured, she never set a timer. She was connected to her food, she knew how much of each ingredient to add and when to add it. In a way, it was like her food spoke to her, telling her exactly how long her dishes should cook and precisely what herb or spice to add.

Who was this woman? She was my Mother. She is the reason I follow the path of the Kitchen Witch to this day. She was a beautiful and amazing woman who pulled herself out of the hardest of times, with a smile and laugh. Cooking was her forte, and it gave her great joy. Remembering her in the kitchen brings me that same joy. As I write this, I feel her presence with me. I am proud and glad she was my mother, and I miss her dearly.

Being a Kitchen Witch doesn't always mean you must wear grand robes, or tons of occult jewelry while you stir a huge pot of bubbling brew. It is more about finding the joy you have for cooking and infusing this joy into your food. It is about finding delight in fresh ingredients, the aromas of your favorite dishes, and the Magick you bring to those who savor your creations. It is about discovering your unique essence that mixes and blends with every ingredient as you create. Of course, if the large pot, grand robes, and jewelry make you feel more connected, GO FOR IT!

I am so happy you have picked up Magick in the Kitchen. This book, as I intend it, is a very practical, down to earth guide for helping anyone connect more fully with your food and the spiritual essence within. I hope that I can help you gain more ground in your spiritual practice by introducing to you how I practice Witchcraft in the kitchen. With a dash of inspiration, a heaping spoonful of dedication, and a pinch of intuition, I plan to show how simplicity is the best method for creating spiritual meaning and abundance.

This book will cover just about everything I can think of surrounding Kitchen Witchery. Magick in the Kitchen is about being practical and sensible. My offerings, ideas, and suggestions are for someone who lives a busy life, and may not have time for complication. In my practice, food and spirituality go hand in hand. This guide will show you exactly how this is possible.

I intend to help you make food more meaningful, far beyond the act of mindless consumption. It is about learning to relate to food in a spiritual way, as I help you see the connection you have to the Elements, and Universe using food and cooking as your conduit. This is where cooking becomes a ritual of spiritual connection and manifestation.

Magick in the Kitchen has taken me a long time to write. I started this book many years ago not realizing there were others out there looking for this type of knowledge and guidance. Truthfully, I never thought I would have the guts or the ability to write down what I know. The task was daunting and many times overwhelming.

You now have the opportunity to benefit from my years of toil, frustration, mistakes, and headaches. OH! Yes, so many mistakes. However, I would not have done it much differently. The bumps, bruises, and open wounds, I endured over the years helped provide me with lessons; valuable lessons allowing me to gain wisdom and clarity. I am also confident, I am not finished making mistakes. I hope that from my tumbles and skinned knees, you can avoid some turmoil of blazing your own Magickal path.

Kitchen Witchery doesn't have to be complicated, daunting, or mind-numbing. Cooking is more than something we do every day that helps satisfy our grumbling bellies. Cooking can be a fun and spiritual experience. I am here to show you how to turn the mundane task of preparing a meal, into your own Magickal tool that will help you develop your spiritual personality and manifest your needs and desires.

This book will help you look at food a little differently and will help you develop a better relationship with food. This does not suggest that you need to meditate with your watermelon or chant with your zucchini, as you establish a connection with food that allows you to become more spiritually connected with the universe. Of course, if you feel the need to meditate and chant with your food, I see no harm in it!

Throughout this book, we will look at developing your own spiritual relationship with food, transforming your thoughts and habits in a practical way. The simple techniques I use will help you create a better you, as you strengthen your mystical practice in the kitchen. The methods and ideas expressed in this book come from real-world experience. I want you to honestly connect with and recognize the spirit within your food. I want you to feel the essence of the sun, wind, water, and earth that infuses your food with a deep connection to the seasons and the universe; a relationship that deepens our own inner understanding of how we show up in the universe. Through this connection, you will discover inner strength and a new delight for cooking. You will find a Magick within your food you have never known before.

Within this book, you will find helpful advice, tips, tricks, and a few recipes to get you on your way to living a Magickal life as a Kitchen Witch. You will learn practical techniques for preparing food, formulating Magickal Intentions, and manifesting these intentions with specific ingredients. You will also be shown the connection food has to spirit, and each element. These connections will deepen your own spiritual knowledge and manifestations. Through my sharing, you will find the bits of information you need to move forward. It is important to remember that your path is your own. I cannot walk it for you. I can only demonstrate to you how I walk my path, with the purpose of giving you inspiration for your own journey.

Please know that because this is a guide and not a cookbook, there will only be a few recipes available. I do offer a variety of recipes on my blog, www.TheMagickKitchen.com if you are looking for more variety.

A Brief History

Writing a history of the Kitchen Witch is like writing a history of Witchcraft itself. Kitchen Witchery is found in the fabric of just about every tradition and has been molded using different methods from many cultures. Although, some feel Kitchen Witchery was established in medieval kitchens where the prying eyes of the Inquisition and other oppressors were unlikely to spy. However, it appears more likely that the term was only coined during this era. It seems Kitchen Witchery is far older.

In fact, Kitchen Witchery is one of the oldest forms of Magick out there. From the beginning of time, humans have known how to construct meals for the purpose of physical nourishment. After all, eating was and still is necessary for our survival. It makes perfect sense that Witches would first learn how to use food in Magickal ways for health, self-preservation, social issues, the benefit of the family, home, legal matters, and so on. More scholars are now dedicating their energy toward learning about the early practices of Witches from many ancient cultures and societies. It is known that women were most likely to be revered in Anglo-Saxon traditions as they were thought to have a more sacred connection to deities and the universe. As historians dig deeper, we learn more about the valuable roles of Witches from all over the world.

Kitchen witchery is not solely a European tradition. If we take a look at Native American traditions, spanning thousands of years, we know that these cultures believed in the Magick of food. Everything had a name and a soul or spirit within. When I look back on my ancestors and their beliefs, I find that food was very sacred. My Cherokee ancestors believed everything deserved reverence. It is because of this belief, respects were paid to food in various ways. My French/European ancestors would also show food reverence and respect. Many to this day continue to believe that food has its own spirit and is deserving of admiration.

As we evolved as humans and learned the Magickal and medicinal properties of herbs, spices, and food - the Kitchen Witch began his/her practices. The hearth and home were the most viable and convenient place to privately conduct Magick. The idea of creating Magick while you cook has its own benefits; beyond convenience. As times and religious views changed, the need for secrecy was crucial, the days of the Witch were fading as Christianity took hold over various cultures. Doing what you can, privately in your own home became necessary.

When I read about the history of Kitchen Witchery and Witchcraft, I put myself in the position of a Hearth and Home Witch; or a Kitchen Witch living in more primitive times. Here is how I sometimes envision our Ancestral Witches as they began their journey of Kitchen Witchery.

It's early morning, and you are up before the rest of the house. You can smell the dampness of the morning outside your small home. It is time to start the fire for the day's meal preparations. You stoke the fire and fill your little cottage with a warm orange glow. When you are cooking over an open flame, you need to reach the desired cooking temperature, which means this fire has to be maintained. This takes time and attention. Once the fire reaches the right cooking temperature, you can cook breakfast. The family eats the meager breakfast and heads off to complete their day's tasks; leaving you to mind the fire, gather more ingredients, prep the food and cook the food. All of this must be done while maintaining the household. This perhaps gives you alone time, an opportunity to learn the Magick of fire and food. The fire having its own specific energy and properties is a critical part of conducting yourself as a Kitchen Witch. You must develop a respectful relationship with fire, and the fire spirits within.

While your fire is burning down to create the right cooking coals, you have a good opportunity to gather some ingredients, and/or prepped your ingredients for the cooking process. This might actually mean going out into the meadows, fields, and forests. Going out alone into nature is where specific knowledge of nature and nature spirits is gained. You develop a keen understanding of how each plant and animal fits into nature's cycle. This time alone in nature gives you an opportunity to recognize its delicate balance. You learn which plants and animals are delicious food, poison and which ingredients are powerful Magick. The art and science of Wortcunning and Wild Crafting are critical elements of gaining knowledge as a Kitchen Witch. You must develop this bond between you and the natural world around you, to do the work you set out to do. We'll discuss this a little later.

While gathering your roots, herbs, flowers, and plants for your meal, you may also hunt. In communing with nature, you learn which animals are tasty, gamy, and meaty. Taking time in nature allows you to know and recognize your place in this delicate balance. You ask permission before taking a life and offer gratitude for the sustenance received. You never take more than you need, after all this is not a mindless killing; instead, it is thoughtful and gracious. Nothing is wasted, and life is not taken in greed.

Once your ingredients are gathered; the plants, meats, fats, and bone have to be cleaned and prepared for the actual cooking process. This also takes time and attention. Making meat pies, bread, roasts, and stews took hours, and during this time the fire had to be maintained. If the coals are too hot, your hard work will burn. If the coals are too cool, your meal will not cook… you get the point. It makes sense that this is where a keen relationship with house spirits, much like the Scandinavian Kitchen Witch poppet and House Brownies became necessary.

As we know from history, traditionally the women of the family would perform the task of preparing meals and maintaining the home. This allowed for the passing of Magickal knowledge, in secret, from Grandmother to Mother and then to daughter. This would also explain why most witches are depicted as female, and more so in the crone stage of life; as Grandmothers would be the ultimate keeps of Magickal knowledge. If you can place yourself in the position of a Kitchen Witch from so many years ago, you can see how practices change as times change. You can get a sense of the deep spiritual importance of food, and the integrity of how food is obtained and finally used.

Let's go back to the idea of how Kitchen Witchery is woven into the fabric of all witchcraft traditions. While not all witches conduct their Magick in the kitchen, the skills of the Kitchen Witch are universal to all paths. The association comes from the construction of recipes. Whenever you follow a spell, you are following a recipe. Whenever you are creating a spell from scratch, you are creating a recipe. You have to know what will work with what, when and how to perform your Magickal technique. Much like cooking you have a process of what to do first, second, middle and last.

Kitchen Witchery helps open the gateway for other types of Magick. Let's open your mind to another great image; you are a Kitchen Witch tending your fire in a small house, and you have some time to kill. Your bones are creating stock over your perfect fire, you have cut your meats, trimmed the fats for later use, your dough is rising, and you have gathered and prepped all your vegetables. Since everything in the home during this time must be made from scratch, you decide to make a doll. But not just any doll, a poppet. This poppet represents a merchant who has swindled your family out of some money. As in most cases, money is a sparse and precious commodity. Money is magick, and this person has used your trust and your money for his own personal greed. He has soiled your good name, without regard for the damage his selfish actions will do to you and your family. Now you are left picking up the pieces of his actions. You and your family are now left to fill the void left by this man's selfishness.

Since the authorities seem uninterested in helping you rectify the situation, you decide to take matters into your own hands. A balance must be restored, and you have the power to influence the energy that will make this happen. You place inside this cloth doll a unique mixture of herbs and plants that will aid your spell. You also place within a strand of this man's hair. (I'm not going to ask how you got it.) When your spell is complete, you rest assured that this swindler will get his just desserts.

How did you know to place that particular mixture of herbs in the doll along with a piece of this man's hair? You gained the knowledge of herbs through Wortcunning and through your work as a Kitchen Witch; passed down to you from your mother. You also learned the wisdom of using something very personal to him through knowing how Magick works. Where did the idea of the doll come from? Perhaps your mother shared notes with a friend who is also a Kitchen Witch, or maybe it is a technique your Grandmother knew. Regardless, the visual representation, and personal effects, combined with specific herbs, words, and emotion… simply WORKS!

Through your many years of experience, you have learned that when your intention is clearly focused the energy, you raise, and the spirits you summon will come to your aide. You never demand to be obeyed. Your requests are gratefully and respectfully bestowed. You know hard work, and you know the value of humility. It is these skills, knowledge, and abilities that you pass down to your daughter(s) once she/they are of age and you feel they are ready. Your willingness to learn and explore blazes a trail for your lineage to follow, leaving your family with a legacy of Magick.

Of course, this is not an entirely accurate depiction of how it would have happened, but you can see the relationship and the probability. Each culture would have its own way of conducting things, and to this day there are many people out there following similar methods.

Living in this modern era, we don't have to make an all day long commitment to maintaining the hearth fire as our ancestors once did. We no longer have to forage for our ingredients or hunt and butcher our own meat. We have supermarkets, farm markets, CSAs, online stores, and Urban Farms to provide us with the ingredients we want and need. If we need to cook a meal that takes several hours, we have slow cookers. When we want to cook over an open flame, we have BBQ grills. Otherwise, we have gas stoves and electric ranges, ovens, and food processors to speed things along.

Most of us choose quick and easy meals for our families, not because we are lazy, but because we are busy. We have many demands being placed upon us each and every day as we maintain relationships, take the kids to soccer practice, volunteer our time, and try to maintain our livelihoods. However, the skills and knowledge of the Kitchen Witch are still practical today, regardless of our lifestyle. The usefulness and tradition of using food, fire, water, scent, and spirit to create Magick will always remain, as long as there are those of us dedicated to the practice.

Business in the Kitchen

Being efficient in the kitchen will make your experience with Magick more meaningful and pleasurable.

Kitchen Safety

I teach teen and adult cooking classes in a variety of settings, to a variety of people. Kitchen safety is the first point I like to make and teach in every class. Knife skills are my first priority, next to food temperatures, storage, and so on.

Every cook should know how to effectively and safely handle a knife while knowing which knife is best suited for the task at hand. Using a knife properly will make your time in the kitchen more productive and enjoyable. Repeatedly, I find that the students with the worse knife skills are the ones who enjoy cooking the least - and for a good reason. We rarely enjoy something when we know we are doing it incorrectly. When we feel our exhaustion or frustration is predetermined, we will avoid and/or dread the task altogether.

Having good knife skills decreases anxiety and fatigue, as you increase your efficiency. I am a great example of this. Before I began teaching teens how to cook I hated chopping, I would get tired and frustrated with my cuts. When I first began teaching teens how to cook, I was required to go through a 6-week training program and certification. A large portion of this program worked on our knife skills. The first few sessions of this lengthy training were focused on breaking bad habits. At first, I was arrogant, and I refused to learn the new techniques. My mom taught me how to cook, and she was a whiz in the kitchen. I thought I knew what I was doing. Then during a training session, the universe showed me how foolish I was. After some time, I became tired, and my knife slipped; I cut myself. Right there in front of kids and parents! It was embarrassing and bloody.

After that, I worked to embrace my training and break my old habits using my knife correctly. Now, I don't know how I ever got through all my years of cooking without these knife skills. It also has explained to me why I would so often feel exhausted after cooking a meal. My efficiency was WAY OFF, forcing me to feel far more tired than I should. Not to forget, my fingers and hands have plenty of scars from not knowing better. I am surprised I even have all my fingers, to be honest! In the years since I accepted my faults and humbled myself to learn proper knife skills, I have not once cut myself.

When you are efficient with your knife, you will chop, dice, slice and mince much faster. I have a bunch of those easy choppers, slicers, and dicers in my kitchen; I never use them. Okay, I take that back - there are two I use because they are far more precise than I am with a freestyle blade. These tools are my Mandolin and my spiral veggie cutter. You know the ones that make noodles out of zucchini and other vegetables.

In fact, my other fancy choppers and slicers are currently packed away in boxes to make room for other tools and necessary kitchen items. Because I learned to use a knife properly and effectively, I have no need for them. I am far faster using a knife when doing basic slicing, dicing, chopping, and mincing, compared to using any of these overpriced fancy tools. There is less clean up too. I only use my cutting board and my knife; leaving me with fewer parts to disassemble, clean, and reassemble.

Beyond knife skills, there are other precautions you should always take when working in the kitchen. I am sure many of them are common sense, but as many of us know… "Common sense is not so common anymore." I will not go into details about making sure you keep your hands out of the fire, and how you should not splash hot oil – or how you should keep hot food hot, and cold food cold. These are skills to be discussed in another book or perhaps discovered in a cooking class.

Even if you are stubborn, like me, you should have the ability to admit that there are areas in the kitchen where you can improve. I love taking cooking classes. Even if I don't necessarily learn something new, they always remind me of the essential basics, we should have a good grasp on in the kitchen.

I want you to be safe. You should want to be safe. If you plan to work in the kitchen, you need to know how to work in the kitchen. Simply said, you need knowledge beyond Magick to practice Witchcraft in the kitchen. When performing Magick in the kitchen, you need to feel at ease so you can focus more on your Magick than your cooking techniques. Taking a few cooking and kitchen safety classes is a very good idea. I have taken plenty and trust me, they are FUN! You meet some great people and learn things you never thought possible.

Magickal Knowledge

Having a good understanding of basic Magickal terms and practices will help you diversify and customize your own Kitchen Witch practice. Look at this book as a stepping stone leading you in the direction of strengthening your own practice. There are many reference materials, books and websites out there for you to sift through. These resources will teach you specific knowledge about herbs, spices, and other essential knowledge. Absorbing this information will take time, but it will add to your knowledge database giving your practice substance.

Some Kitchen Witches like to use stones and gems in their practice. Others like to use specific tools, calling the directions, and so on. I will not go into too much detail about these practices. It is vital that you decide for yourself what tools, and techniques you will add to your Kitchen Witch practice beyond what I offer in this book. As you can see, this is where knowledge of basic practices comes in handy.

Food

If we did not seek out the flavor of foods, we would be content swallowing space age nutrition pills with a big glass of water!

Did you ever notice that food has flavor? Well of course you did!

Flavor is deeply important, and it is what keeps us coming back to the foods we love most – BUT – have you ever noticed something else about flavor? Did you ever notice that when food was grown and prepared with love and reverence, it seemed to taste even more amazing? Maybe it is that special pie your favorite aunt bakes every Thanksgiving? You know the one where she spends a Saturday morning picking out a very specific apple from a local grower. Or your Mother's mashed potatoes, made with butter and cream? Or perhaps the tomatoes you buy at your favorite farm stand?

Food grown and prepared with love, mindfulness, and integrity possesses something special. Its inner essence is soothing and enchanting. Some call it "cooking with love," and I think they are on the right track. Love is a unique ingredient that is not seen. It can't be touched with the hands. Instead, it is felt with the heart and tasted with the soul. When a connection between the four elements and the process of caring for and harvesting food is made, Magick is inevitable.

Albert Einstein knew there was something more to matter vs. energy when he said, "Concerning matter, we have been all wrong. What we have called matter is energy, whose vibration has been so lowered as to be perceptible to the senses. There is no matter."

People like Albert Einstein and Nikola Tesla have been able to prove what mystics have been telling us for centuries. Energy is everything, and this energy is perceived by our mind differently depending on the object's specific resonation of energy. Your food is composed of energy – energy that profoundly impacts your health, Magick, and spiritual well-being. You, your food, and the world around you are all completely connected. But I think you already knew this.

Food Quality
Quality in Magick is a MUST. There is no compromise.

In a nutshell, food is your main Magickal tool. There is sacredness in our food that starts with the soil and Earth. It continues with the refreshment of water, the heat of the sun and whisper of the wind. An energetic vibration manifests itself through the elements, the people who tend the animals and fields, ending with those who prepare the ingredients for Magick and consumption. The quality of the ingredients we use and the quality of their source lends to us a universal energetic vibration which brings its own Magick to our kitchens and tables. In Magickal cooking, we want this Spiritual and Magickal essence intact. To ensure the integrity of our ingredients, we must ensure that our food, spices, and herbs are fresh and whole as often as possible. This also means cutting out and doing away with heavily processed foods. Of course, some processed foods are acceptable as the processing preserves the essence of the food in question. Dried herbs and cooked berries are great examples.

I think Michael Pollan said it best in his book, In Defense of Food: "Don't eat anything your grandmother wouldn't recognize as food." I like to take this further and say we should not eat anything our great-great-GREAT Grandmothers would not recognize as food.

Don't worry, I am not going to turn into a "Nutrition Nazi" to lecture you on what you should and should not eat. I am not perfect in my food choices. I have kids and a active social life; there is no way I can 100% avoid the occasional cheeseburger, boxed mac & cheese, or slice of pizza. Therefore, I cannot judge anyone for their food choices.

However, I will play devil's advocate for a minute while I recognize that personal health is extremely important. Positive health is linked to the quality and types of food we eat. Frankly, my general opinion is that you should eat whatever you want. However, my opinion does change when it comes to something as sacred as Magick. When we talk about Magick, quality is everything. If food affects the quality of our health, it makes sense to believe that it will also affect the quality of our Magick. When we truly consider food, how it is grown and our own spiritual path, we cannot help but realize that the integrity of our ingredients matter. When we work with food and Magick together, Magick will be drawn from the spiritual essence of our ingredients. If that spiritual essence has been damaged or compromised, we will lose much of our food's potency. This is when we must take absolute caution and diligence with the integrity of our ingredients.

I like to follow a few simple rules for self-governing my food choices:

Eat real food.

Buy as fresh as I can.

Buy as local and as seasonally as I can.

Eat the rainbow, (and no, Cheetos are not considered an orange food).

Eat mindfully.

For top-notch Magick, we need top-notch ingredients. Where we get our ingredients and how they are grown, processed, and so on are essential factors. The methods of how our food is grown and raised will undoubtedly cast an imprint of the flavor and Magickal ability of our ingredients. Which is why we should: Choose the freshest ingredients that are as close to their whole state as possible. We must be mindful of the chemicals/pharmaceuticals being used on/in our food, the genetic state of our food, and other questionable industry practices being used on our food.

With that said, highly processed food should always be avoided. The reason I say avoid these foods is because, foods that are highly processed, in most cases, no longer embody or carry their original Magickal properties. Even if the package is labeled "Organic." During the procedure of refining, processing, concentrating, and manufacturing of packaged foods, the specific Magickal aspects we seek have been stripped away through the use of various industrial and/or chemically laden methods. Now, you notice I did not say eliminate. I get that we live in a fast-paced culture and sometimes we just can't find food that is 100% unprocessed. To be honest, some foods are more beneficial after some processing.

In all the recipes I create and offer to you, I use as many organic and whole food ingredients as possible. I don't usually state this in the recipe because it is implied by my style of cooking. This is just how I cook, and honestly, I forget the need to state that I am specifically using organic free-range chicken, or that I use low chemical local apples, as an example. Over the years, I have made it my habit of looking for the best possible whole food ingredients for all of my needs. Also, by me not stating the exact type of chicken, vegetables or what not I use, you are free to use the ingredients that best suit your lifestyle and budget.

Budget is an excellent point to touch on here. To keep things realistic, you should shop according to your budget. I can only dictate how I shop and what I buy - It is not my place to dictate how you shop and what you will buy. The fact is, I cannot walk a mile in your shoes, and I will not judge you for how you shop or what you buy. No one should. You need to be free to determine if your budget and other factors in your life, will allow you to buy more expensive ingredients. Let's face it, organic, free-range, and the like are not very budget friendly to most people. I get this!

If you can't buy the more expensive versions of most ingredients, you should not feel guilty. You should not feel obligated to break the bank over dinner. I know this because I have been there. My family and I have had our low financial points in life, where all we could afford was ramen noodles and peanut butter. Sometimes you have to do what you need to do, to get through the present situation. If you can't afford organic bell peppers, buy the cheaper version, there is no shame in it. Do the best you can, with what you have!

With that said, you have to expect that inferior quality ingredients will lessen the effectiveness of your Magick in the kitchen. This can be remedied by ramping up your focused intention as you cook. Steer your thoughts away from what you lack and bring them squarely into focus on what you have. Perhaps you are really good at creating chants and rhythmic rhymes. Or you are great at singing and dancing. Compensating in these ways may require additional chanting and longer periods of time where you are in a meditative state, or highly focused trans-like state. The point is to use your strengths to make up for any weaknesses.

If you are looking for a way to get better quality ingredients, and organic ingredients at a lower cost, I have some suggestions. There are plenty of choices out there for you to consider. Some are VERY budget friendly and have helped my family and me through some seriously tough times. Let's look at a few options you can consider...

Farmer's Markets and Farm Stands
When you are looking for the best ingredients, local farms are the ideal place to start. While this may not be the cheapest source of fresh ingredients, you will most likely get the best quality. Find a farmer who really loves what he/she does and take the time to develop a relationship with them. This relationship will prove instrumental.

Farmer's markets are in just about every city from coast to coast. These farmers are passionate about growing the best possible ingredients, which will shine through in the flavor of each of their products. Their love for the soil, the seeds, the animals, and the process of growing and raising food is what makes their ingredients so wonderful.

When you buy locally, you can really get to know your local farmer, the food he/she grows, and what kind of chemicals they use, if any. This is important if you are looking to go low chemical and/or organic. Local farmers will also have a better knowledge of what kind of seeds they are planting. They will be able to tell you if the corn they are using is a variety of the GMO sh2 or if the plant is an heirloom variety that is non-modified.

In all the research I have done over the years, I have come to learn some very scary facts about common foods like corn. This self-education has spurred me to do what I can, as often as possible, to ensure the foods I consume are non-GMO. If you have been reading about GMO foods in the media, you know that the long-term testing of these foods is beginning to prove harmful to our DNA, immune systems, and more. Of course, the industry is denying this, but other independent tests are offering scary results. The intention behind the making of GMO foods is a good one. The industry is making corn sweeter, and crops more resistant to bugs and damage. But at what cost? At this point, we do not know for sure, and only time will show us the long-term damage to our health and well-being... not to forget our Magick.

Let's face it, we love our sweet corn. However, there is a repercussion to our enjoyment and demand of sweet flavors. First, let's take a look at how this sweetness came about? Radiation. Yep. Our sweet corn today is a variety that stems from tests conducted using atom bombs. No, I am not kidding. Laughnan, a geneticist, discovered the super sweetness of radiated corn after sampling a kernel for himself while conducting atom bomb tests on a variety of food products and animals. Plainly, genetic modification, meaning it changes DNA. Plant DNA. Animal DNA. Your DNA and my DNA!

After reading Eating on the Wild Side, by author Jo Robinson, I learned that Laughnan, with the help of the Florida Horticultural Society, brought this super sweet corn to the masses in 1961. Now multiple varieties of this radiated corn are the most common variety of corn available in the marketplace. It is estimated that 95% of all sweet corn grown and distributed worldwide is a variation of Laughnan sh2, atom bomb radiated corn. It is shocking to know that from great marketing and questionable science, our diets and tastes have been permanently altered.

So, what? Why should we care that varieties of mutant corn have dominated the food market for decades? Well, it is simple, where we gain sweetness, we lose nutrients like beta-carotene; nutrients that keep us balanced and healthy. This has led us to an overly fed populous with severe nutritional deficiencies. We consume more while receiving less of what our bodies truly need. If we look at this in a Magickal aspect, we lose the essence of the corn. Each kernel has been unnaturally modified. Therefore, it has nearly lost its original Magickal aspects our ancestors recognized.

This takes us back to knowing our farmers and the food they produce. If we can develop a stable relationship with those who grow and raise our food, we can better understand the types of food we consume and use for Magickal purposes. This will also give us the opportunity to demonstrate our desire that non-GMO foods be more dominant in the marketplace.

Local CSA Co-Ops & U-Pick Farms
Here is a great way to get the best possible fruit and vegetables at the cost of a little elbow grease. Let's first talk about the CSA Co-Op option. CSA stands for Community Supported Agriculture. It is usually a small to medium crop producing farm run entirely by volunteers; people like you and me. Most CSAs have several options for their members. You can pay a fee and not have to work in the gardens and collect a weekly bounty of fresh picked seasonal fruits and vegetables. Or you can volunteer to help weed and maintain the garden beds for a set number of hours each week and receive the same weekly bounty. This is an excellent way to get some exercise, garden knowledge, and good quality food for your kitchen. One pitfall that I have run into a couple of times is you don't always have

much control over what you receive. Your weekly share will depend on the weather, harvest schedule and what crops have done well vs. not so well during the growing season. One year I remember for 3 weeks straight our share was loaded with yellow squash and zucchini. I had to become very good at coming up with recipe variations for these hearty vegetables.

My next favorite option that will give you a discount per pound of produce and some exercise are U-Pick farms. Remember earlier I mentioned the low chemical apples I often use? Well, this is how I get them. We have a large local farm market and grocery store that allows people to pick their own seasonal fruit for a reduced cost per pound. If you are a fruit lover like me, you know how quickly fruit can go bad. Picking your own is a great way to ensure your fruit is optimally fresh. The discount allows you to buy a little more than usual. This leaves room for canning and preserving. You can enjoy your hard work for many months to come.

Not only is this economical, but it's also fun. We take the kids, and we pick for about an hour and walk away with a large load of very fresh produce. We start this in late spring with strawberries and blueberries and end in the fall with pumpkins and apples. My kids look forward to it each year. My son especially loves the blueberries. He ends up eating them straight from the bush. We joke with the owners that we should probably weigh him before, and after the trip to get an accurate count of how much he consumed.

Home Grown
To forget how to dig the earth and to tend the soil is to forget ourselves.

- Mahatma Gandhi

This is one I will stress when it comes to food quality and availability. If you can grow your own food, DO IT!

Our ancestors knew that the Earth is a living being and that we are connected to this living being. They called her Gaia, Mother Earth, Earth Mother, and by many other revered names. Today in our western culture, we have lost that connection to the Earth, and her pulsing energy. We have become wrapped up in technology, choosing to remain indoors, rather than go outside and experience her wonders. We have distanced and disconnected ourselves from our Earth Mother. Without realizing our disconnection, we become empty and restless. Nature is a natural healer. It is proven that when we take a walk in the woods or in another natural setting, depression, and anxiety is lifted. Connecting with nature also activates our "happy" hormones. Connecting with Nature through placing your hand in the soil and nurturing life in the soil, is an act of establishing and maintaining personal balance. This act directly reconnects us to the Earth and her harmonious vibration.

Gardening on any scale rejoins us with Earth and the cycles of life. We experience gestation, birth, life, and death throughout the planting and growing season. The act of placing our hands in the soil connects our energy with the energy of the soil, our food, and the Earth. We essentially become part the food we grow. Our essence is sprinkled into every plant straight down to its roots. This essence is absorbed by the plants, to replenish our souls later.

My Cherokee ancestors believe that everything has a spirit - Each plant, animal, stone, even the most expansive valley, all have a spiritual essence. Everything was connected by an invisible mesh of thread, much like a spider's web. In our present time, we have moved far from these ancestral beliefs. We have forgotten the reverence for food and the practices of how food is obtained.

As we sit in our climate-controlled cars, homes, and office buildings, we forget the ebb and flow of nature. We forget how she changes rapidly and slowly. We forget her weather patterns. We forget her desire to provide us with sustenance. Growing your own garden, filled with the bounty of nature is an easy and instrumental task that will reconnect you to the seasons, the earth, and the cycle of life.

Finding your connection to the elements and the cycles of the earth, are important when you seek to conduct Kitchen Magick.

There are plenty of garden options for just about every living space; from container gardening to full-blown urban farming. This is by far the cheapest and the best way to ensure you will have the highest quality ingredients possible. You control the seeds, the harvest, the location, etc. You have ownership of it, and it will take care of you as long as you take care of it.

At my house, we have several raised garden beds, which more closely resemble an urban farm. My in-laws have another 20'x20' plot in their yard, I started for them several years ago. From these two plots, we end up with large harvests each year. We grow just about everything, from purple carrots to herbs and butternut squash. I buy my seeds from heirloom and organic seed companies offering heirloom, non-GMO, and organic options. These kinds of seeds are easy to find these days and provide you the best flavor, color, and quality.

The cost of making your own garden is mostly in labor. If you choose to erect raised beds, then you will have to consider the cost of wood and possibly soil to fill the beds. I use what is called the Lasagna Gardening method, where I use layers of newspaper, cardboard and organic matter to create my own compost that quickly turns into nutrient-dense soil. This method is very cost effective and straightforward, which allows me to save my money for my seeds.

Your first year will always be the most expensive when it comes to your seeds and garden. Once you collect and preserve the seeds from your harvests, each year will become less and less costly. Nature is a wonderful provider. From one seed, she provides you with a plant, which then provides you with hundreds or thousands of additional seeds. All you need to do is put in a little work, and care for your soil and plants. Honestly, I can't remember the last time I bought seeds. We have containers of preserved seeds we collect and dry each year. The only reason I buy additional seeds is to add another variety of fruit or vegetable to my garden. Next year we are considering pumpkins, and I plan to buy 2 different types, one large and one small.

Meats, Dairy & The Like

In addition to growing produce, we should also discuss the options of animal products like meat and dairy. Another huge issue with food today is the unsatisfactory standards of factory farming. Now if you have looked at any of my recipes, you notice I am not Vegetarian, and I am certainly not Vegan. I tried both lifestyles and found that I was better at being a "junk food vegetarian/vegan," which was not ideal by any means.

Instead, of forcing myself to fit into these molds, I decided it is healthier for me to follow my own style of eating. I knew there had to be a better way to get ethically raised, quality animal products without the consequences associated with factory farms. I began scoping out my local butchers and fishmongers and found that they are more than knowledgeable in how the animals are raised, kept, and killed. Much of this is because the animals they process are from their own farms. They care about their animals and take good care of them.

When you buy from a local butcher/farmer, not only are you getting the freshest possible meats and dairy, you are also getting meats that are free from additives like un-natural nitrates. There are yet more options you can consider, like sponsoring a side of beef or pork. When you open yourself up to other possibilities like sponsoring a cow or pig, you have more control in how the animal is raised and processed. This is something my grandfather used to do on his farm. Basically, here is how it works. You pay a specific fee to raise and care for an animal, and in the end, you get either a quarter or half of the animal. I am sure each butcher will have his/her own specifications. The fee you pay goes toward the animal's care, housing, and food while it is alive, and the processing when it is killed.

We did this throughout most of my childhood. All you really need is a large freezer at home to store the meat. Depending on how much of the cow or pig you purchase you could have a freezer full of meat lasting well over a year. Think of how much a single steak costs, you could have 6-10 for about the same price. If you can afford the upfront cost, it is a very economical way to buy ethically raised, fresh, local, and minimally processed meats. This matters in flavor and in Magick. It takes us back to the idea that good quality ingredients produce good quality Magick.

Your Physical Well-Being

Witchcraft is a spiritual experience with physical demands.

It is important to take good care of you, there is no denying it. Your body needs to be in good condition for a variety of reasons, beyond simply looking good. Your mind body and spirit need to be in sync, and you need to feel a sense of vitality for optimal effectiveness. Establishing good health requires regular physical activity, a balanced diet, a positive mindset, and so on. Science is proving this to us more and more each day.

The path of the Kitchen Witch often requires you to establish a certain level of stamina, but this cannot be solely accomplished with a positive and confident mindset. Kitchen Magick requires you to build a certain level of resilience that will allow you to endure the physical demands of cooking and raising Magickal energy harmoniously. This stamina will allow you to raise your energy, chant, and sing all while you cook energetically and maintain your Magickal focus. On many occasions, this has to be done all while standing for extended periods of time. Did you ever notice that you might feel grumpy or irritated after spending a long time in the kitchen? I mean really! All you did was cook! Cooking alone is a physical experience. To keep fatigue from disrupting your physical energy, as well as your mental/spiritual energy, you need to take certain measures to ensure you are in good physical and mental condition.

I can't imagine that our ancestors and creators would want us to feel run down after only a short exertion of energy. The Gods/The Creator gave you everything you need live your best life. Just like everything else, your body will wither and atrophy if not used; leaving us in poor health and with a lack of energy. Fatigue will lead us to do less, doing less, leads us to poor health which perpetuates our lack of motivation and ability.

The only way to combat this cycle of energy loss, and poor health is to move; meaning exercise daily. There is no room for excuses here. I know we like to make as many seemingly viable excuses as possible. "I have no time." "I have no place to work out." "I don't want to be a muscle head." "I hate to sweat," "I don't like exercise," and so on.

Bottom line: If you feel like crap; Magickally, you will perform like crap.

This is why taking good care of you, is critical. In most Magickal teachings, we are taught that you should never conduct rituals or Magick when you are sick or tired. This applies to everyday fatigue. If you are too tired to play with your kids, or too tired to cook a wholesome meal, then how can you expect to raise effective Magickal energy? Regular exercise and eating healthy foods will help you raise quality energy that will lead to potent and effective Magick.

Regular physical activity does not always mean you have to pump iron at the gym, make yourself look foolish with the newest exercise, or spend a ton of money. There are a dozen and more activities you can do on a regular basis that will qualify as exercise. The best part is many options don't feel like exercise. Dancing is a good example and one I like most. I dance nearly every day with a group of other women at my gym. Dancing comes in many varieties, all of which you can do daily or just a few times each week. Some great examples are Zumba, Belly Dance, and Hip Hop. Dance is a social activity that gets my heart rate up and my brow sweating, keeping me in good physical condition.

Please don't feel like you need to jump into a strenuous routine of physical activity to get the exercise you need. Try walking for 10 minutes every day. Then after a couple of weeks bump it up to 20 minutes a day. Walk with a friend and have some meaningful conversations along the way. On nice days when I am not at the gym, I take walks with a very good friend. We like to walk some of the many hiking and nature trails we have here in our town. We spend quality time together as we walk off some unwanted calories and make our physical condition a little better.

What I have found to be true, is that you never realize how much better you can feel, until after you begin to feel better. As I write this, I am a great example. I have been at my sister's house for two weeks helping her through a portion of her medical therapies. I have no access to my gym, and other circumstances are preventing me from doing my daily 60-minute high-intensity workout. I am only able to walk a little each day. After about 5 days, my body told me exactly what it thought of this drastically decreased level of activity. I began to remember what I felt like before I began my regular exercise routine. At about day 5 I began to feel stiff, really stiff. My back hurt and my sleeping patterns were completely off. Now that I am at the 2-week mark of my trip, I notice my muscle tone is changing. The muscles I once had are turning to flab, even my strength is waning. Now that I know how much better my body felt while doing exercise, I am eager to get home and back into my routine.

Now, I'll be realistic. I do a lot of physical activities each day, this is my preference and need. This is not an area where you need to be perfect or do what I do. My wellness requires me to be very active. Because I am a food blogger and author, I must be very active. I eat a lot of different kinds of food on a regular basis, which means I eat a lot of extra calories. I am always sampling new recipes for The Magick Kitchen. If I want to continue doing the work I love, I must keep a very active lifestyle. I don't want you to think you have to fully take on the fitness world to raise your energy level and feel better. Do what you can, when you can and try to make your routine as frequent as possible. You will discover over time that your stamina and health will improve.

Mindset

The attitude you most often emulate has great influence on the quality and outcome of your Magick.

Simply... Energy follows focus!

Attitude is everything in any Magickal practice. The power of your mind will absolutely dictate the outcome of every spell and ritual you perform. If you have a sloppy or poor mindset, filled with uncertainty and negative thoughts, you will have Magick that reflects the same. When performing spell work, you must always maintain the utmost confidence in the energy you summon, and in your own personal energies and abilities. Your power is there. It has always been there, you only need to acknowledge and activate it.

This kind of unwavering mindset comes from intense focus and the accumulation of knowledge and experience over time. Sure, some people are just naturally self-confident. If you are one of these people, great! Get out there and do great things! If you are like I was, you will need to build yourself into a position of inner self-confidence. The good news is that there are many ways you can achieve this solid state of inner control and belief. Most of the techniques for achieving a solid mindset are simple. They only require you to change your perceptions. Many of these perceptions have been formed by external influences, later to become an internal influence. These influences have told us that we are unworthy or that we have no power over changing the results of circumstance. These negative and often damaging influences and messages we have adopted over the years are wrong. You must take responsibility for your path and change the unhealthy perceptions and self-talk you have embodied.

Remain positive

Creating Magick in the kitchen is far more than erecting an altar, being organized, and having good skills in the kitchen. It is about getting yourself in the right place mentally to conduct Magick.

A positive outlook is valuable in manifesting your desires through Magick. Think of where you have abundance instead of deprivation. A worried mind is an obsessed mindset. When we worry, we are desperate to control our Magickal outcomes and future. We are desperate to control manifestation, leaving the universe with very little room to work. In the end, when we deprive ourselves of the infinite possibilities that could be ready and waiting for us.

When we think of our situations with a tone of deprivation, the message we send out to the universe is "Send more deprivation." Depleting messages such as this, most often fill our lives with undesired results while they undermine our true intentions. Take the issue of poverty for example. If you proclaim to others and the universe that you are "so poor," the universe will reciprocate by giving you more poverty.

This is where the mindset of abundance becomes imperative. A mindset to think regarding health, happiness, and prosperity will attract more health, happiness, and prosperity. After all, this is the message you are sending out to the universe. You are a direct link to manifestation, and your primary thoughts must be centered on what you want instead, of what you lack or do not want.

This requires you to mind your thoughts and emotions on a daily basis. In many cases, this will require you to mind your emotions related to certain subjects every minute of every day; until you are able to maintain a primarily positive mindset. In accomplishing this, you find that struggles and life's mayhem are not as bad as they might seem, and, in fact, they are much easier to handle and remove from your life. This requires many people to completely change their attitude from one of misery and complaining to recognizing the positive people and influence in their life. It requires you to become a problem solver, instead of one who wallows in the drama of your turmoil. You must go from seeing the issues with your life to seeing the good things you have in abundance. When we take more time to recognize and appreciate the wonderful things and people we have in our life, automatically we begin to shift our negative mindset to a positive mindset.

Find ways to be confident in yourself. Focus on areas in your life you appreciate. Look at the positive influences in your life you want more of. Focus on the good feelings you receive from the blessings in your life. Perhaps you failed to see the wonderful things you already have in abundance because you took too much time to dwell on the negative. It can be as simple as being grateful for a good parking space, or a discount on that blouse you have had your eye on for some time. Every little thing you can find to be happy over will help fill your lake of happiness and abundance, through attracting more happiness and abundance. This is how we move from attracting the things we do not want, to attracting the things in life we do want.

I made a reference to a lake of happiness and abundance. I like to link or think of intangible ideas in relation to tangible concepts. Often this is done through metaphors I use in meditations and visualizations. Here is a visualization I use when I am refocusing my thoughts from the negative to the positive.

The Lake of Prosperity
This is a quick visualization that will help you focus on obtaining and maintaining your positive mindset. Picture yourself in a small pond. The landscape surrounding you is level and looks as though there once was a large lake here. On the banks, you can see tall willow trees that are withering from lack of water. The lake bed surrounding you is dry and cracking from the heat of the sun. There is an obstructed stream feeding this small pond where you stand. You can only see a trickle of water as it reaches your feet draining into the dry lake bed. You can see in the distance several large

boulders are blocking the flow of water that potentially could fill your pond to its original state as a large lake.

When you look closer at the boulders and rocks, you can see that they are inscribed with words. At first, they might appear vague, smudged, or worn out. Struggling to see, you manage to focus on what is written on these rocks and boulders. Suddenly, you can read what is inscribed. They are inscribed with words and phrases you are very familiar with, like Judgement, unexpected expenses, undervalued, forgotten, hypocrisy, dishonesty, lack of confidence, and so on.

These boulders and rocks represent your own mental chatter and blockages that prevent you from living a happy, abundant, and prosperous life. They prevent you from filling your lake of spiritual progress and awareness. These blockages must be cleared. They need to somehow be broken up and moved downstream allow the water to once again fill your lake. You begin to think of the positive things that eventually dissolve and move these rocks and boulders. In thinking of positive contrasts to these negative blockages, you are able to fill your lake more rapidly. The broken remnants of these rocks and boulders begin to flow and move downstream to help relieve the clog and fill your oasis. Soon, you find yourself able to wade in the water. Before you know it, your feet are lifted from the sticky mud that once held you in place. You become more and more buoyant as your confidence builds. It is not long before the trees become greener, and you swim in deep refreshing waters.

This simple visualization will need to be practiced often as you learn to refocus your mindset. You may also find that some boulders you once cleared reappear as you make new breakthroughs. I don't want you to think this is an instant fix. It is hard to immediately and drastically change a mindset or belief you have carried with you for so long. Limiting beliefs and mindsets that are deeply rooted in your personality, lifestyle and subconscious are the most difficult to eliminate. These influences and thought patterns are like weeds, they are nourished by old habits and denial. They tend to be the most tenacious and difficult to remove, but over time and through your own tenacity, you can completely eliminate the blockages and weeds that hold you down.

Finding your Magickal you

Practicing Kitchen Magick is about finding who you are and emulating who you are through your Magickal style and your food. It is about cooking with your whole spirit and infusing each meal with your essence. This is how universal power flows through you. You become the conduit of potential allowing you to manifest your intentions. It is about how you show up in the universe so that the energy you seek to mold and manipulate, can work with you. This energy does not want to conduct Magickal business with a fake or someone who is unsure of their own power. You must first know yourself and believe in your personal abilities. Everything you need is already available to you, you only need to recognize it and use it.

How do you achieve this? That is the big question. Many never find the answer. The thing is, most Witches have the answer right in front of them, but they fail to see it. They are constantly looking outward for some external remedy or influence that will bring to them the power they seek. My advice to you is to follow your heart. When there are questions, seek answers. Go within as often as necessary and know your higher self. If something feels wrong or off, then find what feels genuine.

We must ask the questions and seek the answers. This is the path of the Witch. We seek truth and knowledge at every stage. Nothing is ever handed to us. This is how we gain the wisdom we need to create powerful Magick. Some toggle from seeker to master, and back to seeker as their needs and path change. This is how we come to know our inner guide and higher self. Your inner guide is part of who we are and will guide you to infinite possibilities. The best way to get to point Z from point A is to walk the path and seek what eludes you. Many times, it is only a matter of placing one foot in front of another.

No, it is not an easy path. Times have not changed much as we remain in an era where we are told what to believe, how to behave, and what we should do and how to think. This is especially true when it comes to right and wrong, moral vs. immoral, Magick vs. reality and so on. You have to sift through all the garbage you are fed to forge your own moral and spiritual compass. Only you can decide what is right for you. Only you can decide what path you should follow.

The path of the Witch is not one that follows the flock. We are not "Sheeple," and if we are to truly follow our own path, we must forge it ourselves. This forces us to think for ourselves, educate ourselves, find mentors who can guide us, and teachers who will share their knowledge. Our path is one of self-education and intellectualism. We must seek to find. The good news here is that we are not alone on this path, and yet we are allowed to remain as individuals. What is right for you, may not be right for the next Witch. This is the beauty of our path. We can make it our own while still being able to appreciate the beauty and influence of diversity.

Creating a Sacred Kitchen

With the right mindset, I know you are ready for this!

Your sacred space, aka the Kitchen, is where it all happens. Your kitchen should be filled with all the elements you need to transcend the monotony of life. Fill your kitchen with symbols that speak directly to you. Encircle it with sacred fragrances that help you relax and feel connected to divinity. Paint it in colors that uplift and inspire you! Make this your space!

The idea is that when you step into your kitchen, you immediately dropped into a state of Magickal or even a meditative attitude. Allow me to elaborate...

Have you ever walked into a place of worship and immediately felt humbled by the presence of divinity? Do you remember how you felt as soon as you crossed the threshold? The feeling of being connected to something bigger than yourself is probably the most prominent. This is the feeling you will want to create within your sacred space.

Claiming your space

Creating the right "vibe" and atmosphere is essential in developing your own inner confidence with Magick. Make your kitchen the place where you take control of the energy, so much that when you invite anyone into this space, instantly their mood will improve. Or perhaps, they will turn and leave your home never to return. It will depend on the person, the intensity of your energy and their willingness to stand in attendance with the Divine.

Yes, I intend to sound a little militant when I say, "Make the kitchen your domain." If the kitchen is going to be your sacred space, don't waiver. Make no apologies or excuses. You have no reason to justify the need for your own spiritual and sacred space. You are entitled to have at least one room in your own home, dedicated to your spiritual practice. The kitchen is the ideal and most logical location for a Kitchen Witch. You should feel no guilt or recoil in this simple justification. If you have any doubt or anxiety, get rid of it now. Any doubt or apprehension will undoubtedly show up in your Magick. If you feel unworthy of the basic right to have your own sacred and spiritual space, where you can practice your religion and spiritual arts, your feelings will taint the Magick you create in this space. Perhaps this is one of the blockages and boulders that need to be removed from the flow into your oasis? As a Kitchen Witch, empower yourself to take the necessary measures in making this room yours.

This doesn't mean you are the only person allowed in this space, but when necessary, unwelcome occupants should be dismissed. It does not mean you have to be rude or overbearing in your demand to claim this space as your own. Instead, this means you should summon your gentle power as a Witch to make this room sacred. This also means you will want to summon the power of Deity and/or the Universe to help you infuse this space with sacred and holy ambiance. Once you infuse this room with the sacred power of Deity and Spirit, all who enter will feel it. This will make some uneasy while others will feel uplifted and energized. Your goal is to create a space so sacred that when anyone enters, they understand that they are guests in the house of divinity.

Still, need more validation? Well then look at it this way. You are the creator of the meals in your home. You provide sustenance and nourishment to your household. It is no small feat. You create the meal plans, plan the shopping list, brave the crowds at the market(s), and/or you tend the garden and grow the food. You are making sure everyone you cook for enjoys every meal you make. You are filling a void for them that they are obviously unwilling to fill themselves. Otherwise, they would be the primary cook. You are ensuring the health and well-being of your household. This should be validation enough for anyone.

Atmosphere

To make this room your own, take some time to think about the atmosphere and aesthetics. Start with color and texture. What appeals to you? Decide what decorations, and modifications you need to make. This room should feel Magickal and comfortable to you. Do you like where the table is placed? Would your space be more functional with a breakfast bar or center island? What about the cabinets? Are they the right color? Could they use some stenciling or re-facing? Or perhaps they all they need is a good deep clean? Speaking of cabinets… Do you have enough storage? If not, can you create more storage, so you have more space to work?

There are plenty of DIY Kitchen remodel and storage ideas on the internet that may help you make your kitchen more functional and appealing. Many of these ideas cost next to nothing and are simply, ingenious. Other options are to look around and see if the flow of your kitchen can be improved by moving things around or reorganizing. If you are looking for ideas, connect with The Magick Kitchen on Pinterest. I have organized several boards that will inspire you.

The Kitchen Altar

The kitchen altar is the first place I stop when I enter my kitchen. Create an altar where you pay homage daily to your chosen deities, ancestors, the Universe, and/or house spirits. This can be a large area of your kitchen or even as small as a box. Personally, I like to hang mine on the wall or place it on a shelf. Not only does this free up room in my small kitchen, but it looks very decorative. I know one Kitchen Witch, who has her altar in a decorative box. This way when her nosey in-laws (who are prone to touching things) come to visit she can close it up and place it on the windowsill or a shelf out of the way.

Every kitchen is different, where you place your altar and how big or small it needs to be will be your own personal determination. After you decide where you will need to decide on the look. Will you change the look to represent each passing season? Or will it have one look and never change? It is entirely up to you.

As I mentioned previously, mine is hanging on my wall. What I did was buy a nice shelf and converted it into my personal altar. I like to change it up every season. In the fall, it is adorned with brightly colored leaves, skulls, and seasonal items. In the winter, I place on it fresh cut evergreen branches and sparkling ornaments. In the spring, I decorate with naturally dyed eggs and bird nests. In the summer, I like Sunflowers and fresh herbs from my garden. Have fun with your altar. Make decorating it an exciting and joyful event.

One more thing to remember with erecting an altar is you must not neglect it. This is a sacred area of devotion to your path and your practice. This is where you pay homage to your patron Deities, ancestors, the elements, and other energies/spirits. This is where you leave them offerings of gratitude toward deepening your connection with their spiritual essence. Neglecting this sacred display would send a very direct, and negative message to the energies you call upon. Your altar should be cleaned and dusted often. Food offerings should be replaced and/or refreshed daily. When you attend to your altar, you are telling the universe that you care and that you are dedicated to your path.

Kitchen Organization and Flow

This may seem trivial, but I find it is extremely important. When you walk into your kitchen how does it look? Is it well lit? Do you have everything organized? Are your most used items easy to reach? Is your kitchen free of clutter and unnecessary items, like loose papers, and appliances (the ones you don't use often)? Are there dishes in the sink, crumbs on the counter, or trash overflowing the can? When you stand at your stove can you easily access your spices, fridge, sink, herbs, pots, pans, and cooking utensils?

When we think of generating the right atmosphere for Magickal work, we might think to add candles, incense, music, trinkets, color, statues, textures, etc. In the kitchen when we do only this, we end up missing something important. This something is the flow and organization of your space. Taking care of clutter and organizing your kitchen is critical to creating and maintaining a spiritual atmosphere.

To take a deeper look into the function of our kitchen (which plays directly into the atmosphere), we need to think of the kitchen's center; the stove. The stove is our modern-day equivalent to the hearth of our ancestors. The Hearth is where everyone would come to keep warm, cook and eat food, and pay homage to patron deities and house spirits. The stove is essential to the flow and function of your Magick Kitchen.

Your stove should be free of clutter, grease, dirt, and empty pots and pans. In many practices, including the practice of Feng Sui, the stove or the Hearth, is considered the Heart of the home. The stove is the focal point for resonating abundance and prosperity. Leaving empty pots on the stove symbolizes and attracts emptiness and deprivation. The stove/oven should be kept clean at all times.

Standing at your stove, let's get a feel for your kitchen's layout, and flow. Take a look at your kitchen and its "work triangle." Wikipedia defines the Work Triangle as follows:

The kitchen work triangle is a concept used to determine efficient kitchen layouts. The primary tasks in a home kitchen are carried out between the cooktop, the sink, and the refrigerator. These three points and the imaginary lines between them, make up what kitchen experts call the work triangle. The idea is that when these three elements are in close (but not too close) proximity to one other, the kitchen will be easy and efficient to use, cutting down on wasted steps.

Most kitchens are already set up to have a good work triangle, it is now up to you (the practitioner) to keep the positive flow of this triangle. On a side note, we can delight in the irony of the coined phrase, Work "Triangle." I am certain designers had no idea of the importance a triangle would have to a Kitchen Witch. The number 3 and the triangle shape are both very powerful Magickal symbols. Sacred geometry teaches us the importance of the number 3 and the powerful influence triangle has on many Magickal arts.

So back to our discussion of creating the right organizational flow in your kitchen. There are a few key points I like to hit before I start any working in my kitchen. These few things are not overly exhausting or labor-intensive, they are actually daily things that can be done without much effort and require little time. How many times have you gone into the kitchen because you found a great recipe you want to try? You are sure you have all the ingredients, and you want to get to work right away. So you look for your mixer or your muffin pan, and they are in the very back of the tallest cabinet, blocked by dozens of other kitchen tools and pans. As you begin moving things around the pans are now falling down on you! Watch out! Attack of the killer kitchen. These kinds of occurrences make our time in the kitchen miserable and frustrating.

OH! WAIT! I have a better example, the STORAGE CONTAINER cabinet!!! Yes, you know that cabinet or drawer, the one with all the mismatched lids, and stacks of storage containers just waiting to leap out at you!!! I would dread looking through the mess of containers and lids because I just knew the entire lot was going to fall out onto the floor in front of me. This used to be an everyday struggle. Eventually, after much digging and cursing, I would find the right lid and container combo. BUT, before I could use the container, I would have to put back the pile of mismatched lids and containers scattered there before me. You would think, I never organized them. On the contrary, I organized them very often… they just never stayed organized.

These are the things you will need to re-evaluate when you survey your kitchen space. Again, there are dozens of storage ideas on the web you can customize to your own needs. This is how I tamed my storage container beast. I tried a few ideas until I found one that worked well in my kitchen.

Keeping yourself organized is not only important for storage and accessibility, but it is also important during the cooking process. I can't tell you how many times I would start a recipe, thinking I had everything, only to discover halfway through, I was out of one or two ingredients. This will not only frustrate you, but when it comes down to focusing on a Magickal recipe, you will no doubt be distracted and depleted of your Magickal focus and energy.

Here is how I solved this problem for myself. Mise en Place. "Misen… what?" Mise en Place (French pronunciation: [mi zã ˈplas]), is a culinary term that means, "In its place". This is the act of pre-measuring and putting your ingredients into designated bowls or on plates making them visible and accessible before you begin cooking. You will often see chefs and cooks do this on TV. They will have a neat little bowl with their pre-measured herbs, spices, oils, etc. sitting on the counter ready to go.

We teach Mise en Place (the act of prepping and pre-measuring each ingredient for each recipe) to the kids who attend our teen cooking programs. This simple act of getting and remaining organized saves your food from over measuring, overcooking, and losing ingredients in the mix.

"BUT, this will add too much time to my cooking process, if I prep and pre-measure everything." Yes, I used to use that excuse too, (she says with a chuckle). I really did think that all this measuring was a waste of time and would make the cooking process go much more slowly. I was wrong. If you look at most recipes, you will see prep time allotted for the recipe. Prep time accounts for the time it takes to measure ingredients and organize them. So, you are not really adding time to the recipe when you practice Mise en Place. You are in fact making your time in the kitchen more productive, and you are preventing additional time spent searching for an ingredient. Not to forget, you are preventing accidents in the area of over measuring and overcooking. Take the time, and practice Mise en Place. Make it a part of your ritual of cooking. Do it mindfully and acceptingly of its benefits.

I found that when I measure everything, this gives me a chance to free up room on my counters and workspace. Because I have everything premeasured, I am able to put away the large bottles or packages of ingredients. Ingredients, I would normally have sat out on my counter, disrupting my work triangle. Before I made Mise en place a part of my regular practice, I found I was pushing aside boxes, bottles, vegetables, etc., just to make room to work. In fact, there had been many times when I knocked over a bottle that was not fully capped creating a bigger mess. Mise en place eliminates this hassle and frustration. You measure your ingredient, you place it in a bowl or on a plate; you set it aside and store what you are not using. Instead of having the entire bag of potatoes on your table or counter, you only have the amount you need for your recipe.

To further ramp up your productivity and efficiency in the kitchen, once you have your ingredients pre-measured and segregated to their own bowls, cups or plates - arrange them in order of how they go into the recipe. This is another frustration and time-saving technique that will allow you to tell if something is out of place or missing. It also is helpful in making sure you add the right ingredient at the right time.

Ritual Clothing – The Magick Apron

Cooking can be messy. Wearing an apron is not only practical, but it can also be an act of spiritual transition.

Sacred or Ritual clothing in most traditions include a robe, tunic, or a cloak – and sometimes a combination of all. The adornment of Magickal and sacred clothing is something I love. Most of us who have studied a Magickal path, know the importance of wearing ritual clothing. The act of putting on specific clothing for a specific purpose gently places us into the right mindset for working Magick and conducting a ritual. As a Magickal cook, practicing Sky Clad is not a very good idea. Ever heard the adage, "never fry bacon while naked"? Well, there is much truth to this. Instead of setting ourselves up for painful burns, we adorn ourselves with a Magickal Apron, much like a ritual robe.

In a Magick Kitchen, the apron is your sacred clothing. Instantly when I place my apron over my head and tie the strings behind my back, something inside me shifts. I am ready to work Magick. I feel the spirit move through me more easily, and I am at ease. Also, I am physically protected from nasty burns and spills.

I love aprons. I have several, and each is different. You can make your sacred apron, or you can buy it. The point is to find or make one that speaks directly to you, and your style of Magick. You can have different aprons for different intentions. Perhaps you want to have one that is red, for when you want to work with fiery energy. Perhaps you have a blue or purple apron that reflects the aspects of water, for intentions related to introspection, meditation, and soothing. Or you can have one apron that is versatile enough to reflect all intentions.

Decorate your apron with symbols, colors, beads, and stones that help you focus and direct your Magickal intent as you cook. Keep in mind you will want to wash your apron from time to time, so make sure that the items placed on your apron are washable. If you want to place items on your apron that cannot be washed, you can incorporate a "secret" pocket. This is a pocket where crystals, statues, and other more delicate items can be placed and removed when needed.

As I mentioned, I have several aprons. I have ones for fun and others for serious business. As a child, my mother taught me to sew, which has given me the ability to make my own Magickal aprons. I have made aprons out of many types of cloth. Some cloth was purchased at second-hand stores and some at the fabric store. I even have aprons made from old ritual clothing I no longer use. Making your own apron gives you the most versatility. You can be more specific about the type of cloth, the cut/fit, textures, and so on. You can personalize your apron and customize it to fit your body type, which is something I appreciate. You can make the neck straps adjustable or the strings extra-long to tie as you see fit.

If you don't have the skill to sew, don't panic. Perhaps you have a friend who can sew. When you ask someone to sew an apron for you, you can make a fun day of it. Take a trip to the fabric store, and then enjoy lunch together. You can even make aprons together if you both seek to practice in the kitchen. Another option is to take a pre-made apron from the craft store and decorate it yourself. Hand sewing requires little skill, aside from patience. If you are unsure of your skill in hand sewing, try using a product that heat-bonds fabric to fabric. The heat activated strips act much like permanent to semi-permanent double-sided tape for clothing. All you need is an ironing board and a hot-dry iron. There are also a wide variety of liquid fabric glues on the market if you want an even easier option.

Tying your Apron Strings

Tying your apron is the first act of your spell work in your Magick Kitchen. Untying your apron is the last act you perform, as you complete your spell.

When I first started Magickal cooking, the idea of tying my apron strings in a specific way didn't occur to me. I would just tie them just as my mother taught me, in a square knot. It wasn't until I began working with sacred knots that I realized I was overlooking some serious spiritual and mystical energy.

Tying knots, in Magickal practices, is most often called binding. When you bind, you are linking the energy you raise to a specific task, object, or even a person. Binding in itself can be its own Magick but can also be used as a portion of all types of Magick. Handfasting is one type of binding Magick of which most of us are familiar.

The knot you tie does not have to be elaborate, and you certainly would not want it to be permanent. Although, in some cases when we discuss or practice Binding or Knot Magick, the binding made is permanent. Permanency is not what we seek here. You have to take that apron off at some point, right? As you tie the knot (this is where the extra-long apron strings play a key role) envision your intention. Envision the energy required for that intention flowing through your fingers and into your apron strings. Then moving to infuse your entire apron. Keep this knot tied during the cooking process. When you untie your strings at the very end of your working, envision that you are releasing any lingering energy of your intention into the universe. This is your last act of Magickal cooking. In many ways, this also acts as the grounding portion of your Magickal working. As you separate the strings from their knots and themselves, you are separating your physical and spiritual body from the energy you have raised. This will leave you grounded and will allow the energy raised to be fully released.

Mindfulness

Drink your tea slowly and reverently, as if it is the axis on which the world earth revolves – slowly, evenly, without rushing toward the future; live the actual moment.
Only this moment is life.
~Thich Nhat Hanh

It is important to be mindful in every aspect. Mindfulness brings us closer to the higher self, the ingredients we prepare, and the food we enjoy. The creator is not your property. The Earth is not yours to own. She does not require your specific existence to thrive and live. She does not owe you her essence, but she readily offers it to you every day. She chooses to include humanity as part of her complicated and interdependent ecosystem. Every moment The Earth, Gaia (or by any other name) is speaking to you through her nourishing gifts and natural beauty. Her presence, her aliveness is in every bite of real food you take. It is in every sip of coffee or tea. She wants you to feel her essence and the care she takes in ensuring you are well nourished. You need to feel her presence, you need to absorb her essence. Without her nourishment, we all wither and die. This is a humbling and magnificent realization.

Your mindset will provide you the right attitude. Your mindfulness will give you a spiritual bearing of which you can use to forge your own spiritual path. Mindfulness is never passive. It is never hurried, and it is always enlightening. When I discuss eating mindfully, I am taken back to my time spent in France. At the time, I was very young and of course, a "Foolish American" according to the French. In my American arrogance, I had no clue the value and the spirit of food. I had no idea what the French have known for centuries.

During my time in France, we ate at various seminaries, restaurants, and even people's homes. To my immediate frustration, everything was served and eaten very slowly. The culture of eating in France is one of celebration and reverence. The French take time with their food. This time and mindfulness offers a whole new layer of understanding and depth to each and every meal. They take the time to talk, taste and savor the experience. They take the time to relish and appreciate their food.

The culture of eating like an American is to hurry up and "Git'r done!" We rush every aspect. We gulp down our food without tasting it. We are crass, gluttonous, and wasteful. I hate to admit it, but this is the view most Europeans have of Americans. We are hurried and unrefined, and this stereotype is given to us for a good reason. Americans blast through just about everything. We can't stand it when we have to slow down even a little. Don't believe me. Test yourself at your next restaurant visit during lunch. A French lunch can take up to 2 hours. The actual eating process takes as long as 30-60 minutes, the rest of the time is spent in conversation. The average American eats in under 8 minutes, and we typically eat twice as much as the French!! If a meal lasts an hour here in America, it is usually because we are with a large group or the service, in our opinion, is slow. In the latter case, we quickly grow upset and complain.

When we rush our eating experience, we are missing something important. We miss the spiritual essence Mother Nature offers to us from within our food. The French know how to savor food, they know food, and they spend a great deal of time relishing in its spirit. This does not suggest that they look at eating as a spiritual act, but the attention they pay, and reverence they have for their food resembles this very closely.

Learning to slow down without rushing through your meals is a difficult habit to break. Here in the US mindfulness requires you to go against the grain of how we have been taught to behave. Our culture demands we serve food quickly, eat quickly, pay the bill quickly, and move on quickly. In our hurried lifestyle, we miss the spiritual experience food offers.

Our food comes from the Earth - the Earth is our mother. She offers us the means of sustenance and well-being. Our deprivation comes only from our societal restrictions and impositions. Eating hurriedly places us in a mental and physical state of stress and anxiety. This does not allow our food to digest properly, and, therefore, we are depriving our bodies (and spirits) of essential nutrients; both physically and spiritually. As we slow down, to connect with our food, we connect with Divinity.

This is another example of why the quality of your food is important, just like your state of mind. Studies have shown that people who slow down better absorb the nutrients in their food. When you relax and take in the experience of savoring each bite, you bring your body out of the "Fight or Flight" mindset. This mindset is where stress hormones force your body to focus on other areas, like your arms and legs taking away focus from your digestion. When you eat your body needs to focus on digestion, not running to the next task. The stress hormones we induce, deliberately shut down digestion, leaving us deprived of the valuable nutrients we desperately need.

My Native American lineage is again, a great example of how people once mindfully focused on food. At one time, my ancestors were one with the Earth Mother and Sky Father and knew their bounty was there for a higher purpose. They recognized that every being that walked crawled slithered and trotted a crossed the earth was connected to one another. So was the act of eating. Their deep connection to the Earth Mother and Sky Father was ever-present in their daily food habits and rituals.

In our modern lives, we have lost our deep connection to the earth. No longer must we hunt, tend our own fields, wait for the harvest, or care for the plants and animals we eat. These acts are most often left to someone else. Someone miles away from us. Slowing down and becoming more mindful of our food helps reconnect us to the cycle of life from the soil to our plates. When we slow down and eat mindfully, we are able to sense the spirit within our food. We are able to reconnect to Gaia, our Earth Mother, and the Universal Creator. When you savor each bite, you can feel the sunshine, taste the falling rain, and feel the nutrients from the soil. You become one with the spirit within each ingredient. You become closer to the natural rhythms of the earth.

There are many ways to regain this sense of spirit within your food. Surprisingly, they are easy. You only have to stop and align your thoughts each time you sit down to eat. One way is to eat outside surrounded by fresh breezes and sunshine. Another is to pay homage to the meal you prepare and eat.

Offering your respects and gratitude
The tradition of saying "Grace," "Thank you" or a prayer before consuming a meal has roots as far back as the beginning of time, and today remains present in just about every culture. My Native American and European ancestors would offer thanks before planting, during harvesting, when hunting, during the cooking process and again before eating. Hunters would ask permission before taking a life and would show their respects to the earth and the animal as they tended to its body. Another common spiritual practice is the act of offering a libation of milk and honey before planting. All of these acts are ones of mindfulness. These simple acts slow us down to recognize our connection with our food and our connection to the greater cycle of life. Through the mindfulness of prayer and gratitude, we are reminded of the spiritual and energetic ties we have to the land. This is where the cycle of life, death, and rebirth is realized and celebrated.

When we slow down to recognize and show appreciation for the food we consume, we instantly transition our mind from "hurry up and get it done" to one of compassion and respect. This mindfulness allows us to savor every aspect of the meal. Showing gratitude reminds us of the value of our food. It reminds us of the static presence food has in our lives. We are reminded of those who tend the crops, the elements working in harmony to grow our food, and the energy expended in producing nourishment for our bodies. This mindfulness takes us beyond physical nourishment to nourishing our soul. Taking time to recognize what it takes to grow something as common as an apple, gives us a new appreciation for the food we place in our bodies. Something we might usually take for granted takes on renewed worth in our everyday routine. Among this, the expression of gratitude connects us to the Magick within our food, which then leads to a deeper connection to the Magick within ourselves.

Food is something we cannot live without. Today, the experience of eating has become a mindless rut; a drone like – monotonous habit. We have forgotten how to taste our food and really live the experience of eating. To reconnect with the energetic essence of your food, you will only need to slow down and take the time to recognize your food. It is a simple shift of acknowledgment taking on the attitude of respect and gratitude for yourself and the natural world around you.

Daily Devotional to Mindfulness

I usually wake up before the rest of the house, and I head down to the kitchen. Making coffee is often first on my agenda. As I open the coffee container, the aroma of roasted coffee beans fills my nose. The fragrance excites my soul. It's no secret, I LOVE coffee (and tea) - most of all the fragrance. Carefully, I count out the right number of scoops to make a full pot, then set the grinder in motion. The noise fills the kitchen alerting everyone that the morning has begun. I pour the water, glistening and trickling into the coffeemaker. As I pour, I take notice of the freshness and purity. After switching on the coffeemaker, the gurgling begins. Eagerly as the last drop falls into the carafe, I snag the pot and pour myself a large steaming cup. The steam rises and swirls, it wafts and disappears.

Depending on my mood, I measure just the right amount of sugar, and milk and watch how the milk quickly changes the coffee to a light color with pillow-like swirling clouds. I stir my coffee slowly allowing all the flavors to mingle. While the kitchen is still quiet, I hold my steaming mug in my hands and turn to the North. I hold my cup to the North, and fill my mind with thoughts of the shady groves where the coffee was grown, and the soil that nourished the plant. Making a one-quarter turn to the East, I think of the wind that gave a lift to the bees and other pollinators' wings, allowing the coffee plant to flower and flourish. Making another quarter turn, I face South, where I am reminded of the warmth of the sun that gave the plant the ability to grow and create energy in the form of photosynthesis. I make a final quarter turn to face West, where I am filled with thoughts of the gentle rain that helped hydrate and wash nourishment to each bean. Raising my head to the sky, I acknowledge spirit, the merging of all four elements that brings balance to the flavor. The balance that allows me to fully enjoy the flavor of my morning coffee.

This is an example of a simple morning devotion you can perform each day, with any beverage you choose. You only need to take time with it and experience the beverage. When I say experience the beverage, I mean fully. Immerse yourself in the making or brewing of your favorite morning beverage. Take time to appreciate every aspect necessary to bring this beverage to your kitchen. Take time to appreciate and delight in the process that allows you to drink and enjoy this beverage. This will open you up to new understandings and perceptions you might have previously overlooked.

Performing a morning devotional related to your path, your patron deities, the elements, etc. is a great way to solidify your spiritual mindset and mindfulness each day. You can conduct a simple mantra, or just be aware of every motion, the sounds, and fragrance related to your morning breakfast rituals. Remember that simplicity is sometimes the most elegant and meaningful ritual. I am sure your mornings are just as hectic and busy as mine, you don't have a lot of time to cast a circle, pray, meditate, ground, center… so on and so forth. This is why simplicity makes a spiritual life attainable for people like you and me. You don't want to feel rushed through the process of creating mindfulness or become distracted. Take a few minutes to fully appreciate and ingest your morning coffee as you connect to your higher self. This might mean you get up a few minutes before everyone else in your household or finding a quiet place away from the morning rush. Make this practice a part of your daily routine, and you will notice the difference in your connection between spirit and food each and every day.

Adjusting Old Habits – Learning to Eat Mindfully

Make each bite a small, deliberate and mindful act of connecting with infinite spirit.

If you are a fellow American or if you lead a fast-paced lifestyle, I know this will be a tough one for you. At times slowing down is still tough for me. Like I said before, it is hard to buck cultural training and the habits/expectations you have followed for many years. The process of changing the habit of eating too quickly will take a lot of discipline, patience, and time. I will not lie, it is a challenging journey to slow down when you live in a culture or lifestyle of "hurry up and move forward."

Have you ever eaten an entire meal, and at the end wondered where all that food went? In times like this, we are too preoccupied with the world around us or the endless chatter in our heads, rather than fully experiencing our food. We are concerned about the day's mistakes, the driver who cut us off in traffic, our social capabilities, or the disaster your boss was furious over today at work. Mindless eating prevents us from truly knowing what our bodies need. Mindless eating also prevents us from knowing exactly how much food our bodies need. In America, we have a habit of eating the serving sizes we are served. The old adage, "Clean your plate" is very dominant in many families. On top of this cultural teaching, we eat in front of the TV, the computer, in the car, and on the go. This is where our supersized portions show up on our waistlines and medical charts. Honestly, it is our own fault. We demanded more, and restaurants provide. We convinced ourselves that this lifestyle is more efficient. It is about time we slowed down and really looked at the benefits of this lifestyle. What have we really gained, besides heartburn and larger clothing sizes?

Slowing down and eating mindfully is essential in reconnecting with the spiritual essence of our food and the spiritual essence of our higher selves. Slowing down brings you back into rhythm with the Creator and the universal energies. It is essential in recognizing the needs of your body... the true needs of our body. Slowing down helps us realize and relish the beauty of the food we eat. When we become mindful, instead of mindless in our eating habits, we connect to the fields, the sunshine, the air, and the sun where our food was grown and raised. Eating mindfully helps us make better food choices and helps us eat more compassionately. Eating mindfully allows our stomach and brain to communicate cohesively, enabling our head and stomach to accurately register fullness. You begin to taste your food and relish its uniqueness. It takes about 20 minutes for your brain to realize that your stomach is full. Many times, we overeat because we are not allowing our head to be part of the eating process.

When I began eating mindfully, I quickly realized that many of the foods I was eating on a regular basis were actually disgusting. I hated the flavors, but because I was culturally expected to enjoy them, or because food advertisers proclaimed it was "delicious," I would eat them. Some of the foods were highly processed and not good for me at all. As I began really tasting and connecting with my food, I realize that I was eating all the wrong things. I didn't discover this because the new diet trend or nutrition magazine told me so, I figured it out by listening to what my body really needs and wants. Looking back, I realize that some of the reasons why I was eating so quickly was to get the experience over with. Eating these foods quickly meant I would no longer have to eat whatever was on my plate. Now I that know l what my body wants, I am able to truly enjoy my food. I know what foods will serve me best and these are the foods I enjoy most. These foods are fresh and delicious. I had no idea what I was missing until I re-evaluated and then adjusted my habits and perceptions.

Remember France? While I was in France, I had to learn to eat slowly which lead me to eat more mindfully. Although the transition was difficult, I am glad for it! Being in an environment that expected me to slow down, offered me an advantage to learning this new habit. Your environment plays a large role in your habits and your ability to change them. Once I left France for the States, my old habits returned quickly. Even today, after nearly 30 years, I still find myself falling back into the habit of eating too quickly and carelessly. I find I have to be extra diligent in my pace when I am stressed or when we eat at restaurants with family. The good news is this, if you really want to accomplish change, you will. I also know that if I can do it, you can too.

I would like to offer to you a simple exercise that will help you practice mindfulness while you eat. This exercise begins when you sit down to eat. Whether you are sitting in a restaurant or at home, this exercise can be done anywhere. This exercise is based on your first bite of food and will help set the tone for your entire meal.

Eating Mindfully Exercise
Before you sit down, take a look at the table. Take in the atmosphere of the room. If it feels high energy allow yourself to feel joyful. If it is mellow, allow yourself to feel relaxed. Keep a positive attitude as you sit and order and/or wait for your food. Once your food is served, you will want to draw your attention to your first bite of food. Take a deep breath. Look at the presentation of the food. Look at the arrangement of the table, the décor, and once again notice the ambiance. Inhale the aroma of the food. Look at the colors and textures placed before you. Take in all you see. Is your plate filled with a variety of colors? Can you see the seasoning? Does the food look appetizing? Is there sear or grill marks on your food? Can you sense all the layers of flavor set before you?

Now, choose your utensil and select a small bite from your plate. This first bite should be a mixture of every element you can feasibly gather on your fork or spoon. A salad is a good example. Take a bit of the lettuce, some of the tomato, a little dressing, and some of the protein. Now, take your first bite, and stop. Set your utensil down and allow this first bite to sit in your mouth a moment. Taste all of the flavors together. Now slowly begin to chew. Savor each ingredient as they mingle together. Notice how when you begin chewing, the flavors might have intensified or changed. Think of the farm where the fruits, vegetables, nuts, herbs, and spices were grown. Think of the chef, or cook who prepared your meal. If the cook is you, think of the techniques you used to prepare your meal, think about the care you placed in choosing the ingredients. Think of the time someone put into developing the recipe. Think of how many times they tested the flavors to ensure the recipe was suitable for your table.

Think of the sun shining down to grow your food. Think of the water that refreshed and hydrated it. Think of the wind and breezes that rustle the leaves and cooled your food on warm summer days. Think of the rich soil where your food grazed and grew. Think of all the workings of Nature as she mixes and mingles each element to bring beautiful balance and flavor to your palate. Without the cooperation of all four elements, you would not have this meal to enjoy.

Fully chew (about 15-30 times) and swallow your bite, before picking up your utensil for a second bite. On your second bite try only one ingredient, and savor it in the same way as your first. Do this with all the ingredients you can find on your plate until you are back to eating the combination of ingredients in one bite. On your plate, if you have lettuce, carrot, onion, and egg – try them all individually then go back to eating mixed bites. Are some ingredients salty while others are sweet? How do they mingle when brought together? Remember to sip some water in-between bites. This is a great way to cleanse your palate, before tasting new flavors. Even as you sip your water, feel it refresh your palate and quench your thirst.

This mindful eating exercise is what brings our physical body into communication with our mental and spiritual bodies. Our brain is able to fully experience the process of registering each bite as we take it. Our spirit is nourished by our attention to detail. Through this, we become aware of the connection we have with food and the Elements, Magick, self and the creator.

The Elements in Kitchen Magick

In my little rendition of how Kitchen Witches got their start, I mentioned that knowledge of the element of fire being crucial to practicing as a Kitchen Witch. I didn't give you all the information. There are of course 5 elements. In some traditions, there are as many as 7 elements in Magick. We have the traditional Earth, Air, Fire, Water, and Spirit (making 5) or if separated Spirit out you have: Above, Below and Within making 7 elements. You get to decide the number of elements you will work with.

These elements correspond to our journey in many ways. When we think of the elements, many of us think of the cardinal directions and how they correspond to the rising sun to flowing waters. Many also associate the elements with the seasons and the cycles of life. We all have our own ebb and flow. There are times of harvest, times of planting, times of bounty, and even times of deprivation. As with the wheel of the year, we are ever changing and always moving, this is where the elements become an important association. Each element has a lot to teach us about ourselves, as well as living in harmony with the Earth. Most importantly to us, as we indulge in the knowledge of Kitchen Witchery, the elements play a part in teaching us about food and the Magick within.

It is important to remember that not anyone plant or animal will only house within its essence one single element. As we know nothing can survive, without all the elements being present, as they work together creating balance. This means they must all mingle with one another to create and sustain life. Of course, you will have one element that appears to be more dominant than another, but keep in mind that every element is present, making up nature's delicate balance. Let's take a look at the elements and how they show up in food, the cycle of life and Magick.

Earth

Earth will orient you with the solid items you use and rely upon for Magick. Examples are the ground beneath your feet, the soil that gives plants stability, and the wooden spoon in your hand for stirring. You can associate Earth most strongly with North, your earthy vegetables or root vegetables. Specific root vegetables you may associate with the element of Earth are potatoes, carrots, parsnips, and beets. Mushrooms are also placed in this category as they are often referred to as having an "earthy" flavor.

Earth is about receiving harvest and bounty. This is the time of our life when we have things in abundance, and this can be anything from monetary wealth to happiness, food, and/or the presence of family and friends. In a spiritual sense, this is a time of accepting the knowledge we have gained. It is time to use knowledge and experience to create wisdom. The message of the earth is, "plant yourself and grow."

Earth is associated with North, mountains, forests, and lush green landscapes. Earth is stability, security, and sustainability. Earth is nourishing as we harvest the fruits of our labors, both figuratively and physically.

Air

Air will show its importance during the creation of recipes, spells, and in the planning of activities or goals. Foods associated with Air are often the herbs we might burn like sage and lemongrass. Light and leafy vegetables like lettuce are also associated with Air.

Air is present in the aroma of food. It is the floating and flitting essence of every ingredient and meal you create. It is the scent of apple pie baking in the oven or the scent of freshly brewed coffee. Air is creativity, the inkling of an idea, the birth of a project. Air is usually associated with East. Our spiritual time in Air/East is when we are collecting knowledge. We are eager to learn. The mindset of Air is often flighty and distracted. It is a time when we realize there is so much out there to learn and experience, and we are eager to take it all in. Air is a time to seek and conspire. Spring and new beginnings are best associated with Air as we plant the seeds of change and create a bounty for our literal and spiritual lives.

Fire

Fire is action and passion. It is heat and motivation. Fire will move you to change. Fire is collaboration and focused movement. Fire is where we gain experience. Foods associated with fire are usually spicy and awakening, these foods include hot peppers, cinnamon, garlic, and ginger.

Fire is associated with South and Summer. It is where we learn to take action, and we work hard toward our goals. The ideas and goals we have planned are ready for motion, and fire is what gets us moving to make things happen. This is the state I notice most Pagans think they should remain for the entirety of their spiritual path. It is easy to forget how the wheel must turn, to maintain balance and comprehension of the path we tread. Yes, Fire is where we get things done, but we cannot expect to always remain in this state. Too much time spent in Fire and we will burn, or rather burn out. Sound familiar?

Fire is where our projects and ideas grow and mature. This is the Summer of our journey, where we are surrounded by growing gardens. It is time for maintaining these gardens (figuratively & literally) to keep them free from pests, disease, and other unwanted things like weeds or negativity. This is our maintenance stage where we learn to keep up and spread ourselves evenly between projects without spreading ourselves too thin.

Water

Water is flexibility, inner knowing, and patience. Water is associated with West, which is also a time of rest, reflection, and meditation. Water reminds us to be patient with the harvests. On all spiritual journeys, there is a time for stagnation and rest. This is time for reflecting and meditating on what we have planted, grown and harvested.

Some of the foods associated with Water are grape, plum, melons, and strawberry. It is the stock made from bone, and the tea in our cup. Many foods associated with Water will be very juicy or induce relaxation and sleep. I see many Pagans developing an issue at this stage in the spiritual journey. I include myself in this. We tend to forget the importance of this is a time for reflection and meditation, rest and patience. This is where ideas and clarity are known. We tend to feel like the break in our learning and growing is harming our journey. Instead, we need to rest a while before we can move forward. This rest period keeps us from overwhelm and burning out.

Spirit
All encompassing. All inclusive. This is the entire meal on your table and plate. It is the ambiance you create, the food you present and the state of mind you choose when you sit to eat. It is the accumulative result of your primary mindset and presence in the universe.

Spirit brings the entire journey together. All the elements and the directions are one. Spirit is all foods and is the state of satisfaction when a balance is created. Just as the wheel is ever turning, we may not remain in the state of Spirit for an extended period of time. In many cases, we only catch a glimmer of spirit. That moment of complete clarity before we are returned to our mundane mindset.

One thing to remember about spirit is that it is the balance of all the elements and every action and thought pattern we embody. This balance is something that changes as we change. Balance has to be continually adjusted and readjust as we encounter new experiences, and influences in our spiritual and mundane life.

There you have 5 elements to work within the kitchen. You can feel free to break the elements up as you choose. If you like to work with more than the 5 elements as discussed previously, feel free. This is your journey, and you are free to do as you choose.

Finding the Right Ingredients

Wortcunning is a long-respected tradition. What the heck is Wortcunning, you ask? I know this is something most people ask when I use this word. Wortcunning is not something that comes up in everyday conversation. Simply put, Wortcunners are people who understand plants.

Wortcunners are the wise women (and men), who truly understand plants, in all aspects from medicine, to preserving, to the mingling of flavor. Wortcunners don't stop there. They know the identity, Magick, and lore of plants, how and when to use them; along with how to plant, tend and harvest them. Wortcunners know the "spirit" of the plant and see beyond what most only see with the naked eye.

Previously, I mentioned the importance of knowing your food and ingredients. This goes beyond where it was grown, the variety, and if it is organic and/or heirloom. You will want to know as much about your ingredients as possible. The Kitchen Witch is typically well versed in the knowledge of their ingredients, and for a good reason. The Kitchen Witch must know when, where, why, and how to create powerful Magick. This wortcunning knowledge comes with time, education, practice, and patience. There is a lot out there to absorb. I always recommend making life simpler by hanging quick reference charts in the kitchen or keeping them in your Book of Shadows for easy access.

How do you know what recipe and ingredients to choose?

I have interacted with many Magickal cooks over the years. I have seen things done a dozen and one different ways. Some cooks spend a great deal of time researching each and every ingredient that goes into one Magickal Recipe. Some section foods into basic groups like Earth, Air, Fire, and Water. These methods are what work for these cooks. To me, these examples limit you in a variety of ways.

I like to find a happy medium. I also like to be practical, because I lead a busy life. To research and analyze every single ingredient in recipes tends to frustrate me. When you get down to it, the process is just cumbersome. After spending a great deal of time and energy on research, I simply don't have any energy left for cooking... much less raising Magickal energy. In the end, I throw out half of my ingredients because of their "presumed" Magickal contradictions. Not only does this become infuriating and overly analytical, but it disrupts the flavors of your meal. In the real-world, this process is simply too much hassle!

In contrast, when you place foods and ingredients into too few categories, they become overly simplified. You limit the versatility of your ingredients. This method tends to cut off some of their alternate personalities or Magickal aspects. A good example of a versatile food/ingredient is Cinnamon. Cinnamon is well known for its attributes related to Power, Success, and Lust, but these are only a few of its Magickal attributes. If we place Cinnamon solely in the category of Fire, we would be missing out on some of its best aspects, like Spirituality and Psychic Ability/Power. This is where the knowledge of the foods you plan to use (wortcunning), comes in great use. When you know the versatility of your ingredients, you can use them to your advantage in a variety of ways. However, this seems to be where some confusion and frustration comes into the mix. When attempting to perform spell work while cooking, I want the most "bang for my buck!" This also means I need a process that is logical and practical. To accomplish this, I need to eliminate unnecessary obstacles and restrictions.

Here is what I do. I find this to be a very easy and effective method, which gives me more flexibility in Kitchen Magick. I choose 2-3 (sometimes as many as 5) dominate ingredients for my focus. These few ingredients will carry my intent for the entire spell. This way I am not boxing my ingredients into too few categories, and I am not complicating the recipe by being overly analytical. All my other ingredients are there for flavor, texture and/or functionality. There is no need to over think the process! I often find that most existing recipes will already incorporate complimentary ingredients.

A good example of my methods is in the use of salt & pepper. Every recipe requires salt, and most require the use of pepper at some point in the cooking process. Salt is a very good cleanser. Magickally we would use it to strip energy from objects, atmosphere, and self. But we would not want to strip the energy away from a spell we are attempting to perform. It would be counterproductive to remove the Magick we are seeking to raise. We also cannot leave the salt out, unless you are willing to sacrifice flavor. So in most cases when I cook up Magickal recipes salt has only one job, flavor.

Next, we look at Pepper, which is also another powerful ingredient. Pepper is often used in spells related to protection and exorcism. Not every recipe we create will have the intent of exorcism and/or protection. We do, however, need flavor. It is in these cases that the Magickal attributes of Salt and Pepper are voided by our own Magickal focus. This is where our mindset balances the energetic weight of the spell. Our primary ingredients will help us hone our focus. This is why only choosing a few ingredients is effective. During the ritual of cooking, you will raise the necessary energy using your primary ingredients; like invoking your intended Magickal outcome.

When you know as much as you can about your ingredients, your knowledge will make Magickal cooking more flexible. This method will more readily and easily help you match recipes and ingredients to your specific Magickal needs.

Intentions come first

Always remember, your purpose for any spell work comes first. Let me give you an example: I intend to calm anger or chaos in my home. Since Wortcunning (the intimate knowledge of food, herbs, and spices) gives me the ability to choose the right ingredient, I know I can choose Basil as my main ingredient for my recipe. Basil is perfect for soothing tempers and chaos in a variety of settings and can be used in many different ways. Next, I look for a recipe that features basil as one of the ingredients, if not the main ingredient. Pesto sauce! Perfect!

This particular mingling of Magick and food can be as simple as replacing my tomato sauce with pesto to create a simple pasta dinner everyone will enjoy. After all, pesto is mostly Basil, and Basil is the ingredient that best suits my Magickal needs. My next ingredient of focus in this recipe is garlic. Garlic is a great protector, and I will use its potency to create a protective barrier, once Basil has done its job. This formulation creates less fuss in your Magickal workings, allowing you to become more productive on a busy Thursday evening when everyone is cranky and demanding dinner! This "no-nonsense" real-world, practical approach grants you flexibility. You will feel more empowered to do what you need to do on a Magickal level at any time, and (this might be most important) you will be able to cook delicious food while configuring effective spell work. The few ingredients you choose as your focus ingredients become your superstars of the spell, relieving you of the overly tedious task of analyzing and research leading up to the act of conducting Magick.

Tools & Gadgets

There are few special gadgets or items you need to buy or own to make your life as a Kitchen Witch more effective. In most cases, things are just things. Your mindset and ingredients are what get the job done. However, there are a few important things you should always have. These tools and gadgets just make life in the kitchen more efficient and less stressful. Some items also speak to our spirit and joyfulness. These items help you feel good in the kitchen. Let's take a look at some of the items you might want to have present in your kitchen at all times.

The right cookware and tools

One thing I have always been fussy about in the kitchen is my cookware. When I look for pots and pans I look for the highest quality I can afford. Do yourself a favor and refrain from buying or using flimsy aluminum pots and pans. Not only will they not last you more and a couple of years, but they are also bad mojo. Instead, find heavy bottom stainless steel, Earthenware, copper and/or cast iron. In the long run, you will thank yourself! Now, cast iron and professional grade heavy bottom cookware is not cheap, and that is for a good reason. This kind of cookware (when properly cared for) will become something you can pass on to your kids and possibly grandkids. They become a valuable Magickally infuse heirloom your family can enjoy for many years to come.

Next, get yourself a good set of kitchen knives, cutting boards, and basic kitchen gadgets; like a garlic press. Again, they will not be cheap and for a good reason. When you buy high quality, they will last you a very long time saving you frustration, and money in the long run. When you care for them properly, they will endure the test of time. They are also made of quality materials that lessen energetic interference that damage and obstruct the flow of Magick.

Just a note: Remember to have your knives sharpened every few months or years depending on their frequency of use. Sharp knives are very important and will help avoid accidents.

The Kitchen "Wand."

I have to face it, I don't like wands. I never use them and could never justify to myself why I need to use one. To me, the use of a wand was more of a crutch and something the Wiccan authors put into use as "fluff" for the practice of Magick, voiding the true purpose. To me, the use of a wand showed to me the lack of faith Wiccan teachers have in their students' ability to direct Magickal power. I am sorry if you don't feel this way, but I just can't justify their need or usefulness in Magick. If you read my blog, you will notice I rarely if ever mention them. As a Kitchen Witch, the use of a wand is cumbersome and (to me) not necessary.

However, wooden spoons are a different story! They are useful and can be permanently decorated to represent your style and Magickal personality. I will not use a wand, but I have several Magickal Wooden Spoons I use frequently. As a Kitchen Witch, if you insist on using a wand, I highly recommend a spoon over the traditional wand in the kitchen. There are plenty of good vendors out there who make and sell Magick Kitchen Wands. These wands are beautifully decorated and safe to use. If you cannot part with your traditional wand, make it more of an altarpiece. This will leave your hands free to cook in the kitchen, rather than fumble with too many tools and objects while your spell work burns.

Storing Magickal Recipes

After you have made your Magickal recipe and you have eaten your fill, what next? Do you toss away the leftovers? If you do what happens to the working. Can you store them? What if they spoil? What should I do?

When you make Magickal recipes, you will want to savor every bit of flavor and reap every Magickal benefit! But there is a time when you cannot eat another bite! You have invested your time and energy into your food, and you should take the necessary steps to care for your working when the meal is complete. Since we live in the real world, you have real-world options!

In my practice, there are about four options when it comes to dealing with Magickal leftovers:

1. You can fully consume what you make, meaning you will only make enough for one meal, without stuffing yourself like it is Thanksgiving Day!

2. You can store the leftovers for consumption later. Hopefully by the next day.

3. You can compost or burn your leftovers

4. You can toss them

The choice is yours. I try very hard not to throw out any Magickally infused foods. Which means I never throw out any food I create. To me, it's just bad Magick to throw out your working. Instead, I choose to consume it or compost it.

Storing leftovers in your basic glass storage container is ideal for when you simply cannot eat all the food you cook. Just be sure to use the leftovers within a day or two. Some recipes can be frozen but beware of freezer burn. Freezer burn can and will destroy food as well as its Magickal charge.

What to do with Spoiled Magickal Recipes

First, try very hard not to allow your Magickal food and workings to spoil. There are a few exceptions to this rule, but when it comes to most things, you should avoid the deterioration of your Magickal work. When you follow Kitchen Witchery as a spiritual path, and when you heavily consider it, spoilage is blasphemous. You are sending the universe a direct message saying, "I don't really care about my workings or the results." As Witches, we know there are consequences for every action and non-action. This is the flow of energy. How we treat people, things, ourselves, and our Magick sends a very direct message.

While we may try very hard to prevent spoilage from happening, no one is perfect, and things sometimes fall through the cracks. Somehow, that one container of food gets hidden in the very back of the fridge, where the Spoiled Food Faeries have their way with it. When food reaches the point of spoilage, it is time to dispose of it. This is when you need to decide if you will toss your spoiled Magickal working, or compost it. You could also burn or bury it if you have the means. But in remaining practical, we will consider the options of tossing it or composting spoiled Magick.

Finding appropriate ways to deal with these incidences is not only good problem solving but demonstrates to the universe that you care about your workings and the energy you raise. Remember this working is part of you. You would not readily toss yourself away, so you should not be willing to do the same with your own Magickal Creations.

Composting is my preferred solution compared to tossing my Magickal recipes. Composting is easy for me and beneficial since I have a yard and garden to feed. Many products on the market will help you do the same. You can buy a compost system that does most of the work for you. They come in a variety of sizes from very small to extra-large. Most are well designed and durable making their long-term use possible and efficient.

In my yard, we have room for a large compost pile. My compost pile is contained by long pieces of wood, creating a large box where our kitchen and yard waste is turned into soil. It is very basic and did not require us to erect a large caged structure or take up half the yard. It requires little attention and yields beautiful soil, often called "Black Gold" for our gardens. If you have space, I recommend this approach. The internet is stocked full of compost instructions, and infographics that will help you learn to compost your food correctly. There are even methods for composting indoors, believe it or not! Just do a simple search on the internet, and I am certain you will find what you need.

When I compost my Magickal leftovers, I like to say a little prayer as I create an offering to the earth that will, in turn, be made into the soil for my garden. This act of recycling allows the earth to turn spoiled Magickal energy into something that will nourish the garden. Composting allows the energy to re-invent itself just as nature intends.

Here is a simple prayer you can perform when you compost Magickal foods.

To the Lady of Darkness and the Lord of Light, I return to you this Magickal plight.

Energy raised and waning fast, I give to you what once was cast.

Rejuvenate and restore: return Magick to me once more.

Ethics

This is always a touchy subject, as we all have different ethical and moral compasses. Many believe Magick should never be used on anyone without their specific knowledge and permission. Others feel Magick should never be used for personal gain. These are only a couple of ideas where I see the most conflict in many Pagan forums. As a Kitchen Witch, we often run into the question of ethical and moral boundaries.

Let's look at using Magick for personal gain. I take my lessons from nature. Nature gives us bounty where ever we go. You plant one seed, and you get a thousand in return. Nature is telling us that she wants us to be well cared for, and to live a prosperous life. She also tells us that to obtain this bounty we must work for it. We must put forth the necessary means (energy) for reciprocation. Nothing is free, and the law of Equivalent Exchange is ever present. Magick is the essence and vibration of Nature and the universe, it only makes sense to me that we use this energy to live prosperous lives.

Let's look at this in an economical way. I like to use money and economics as an example because it is an area in which we can all relate. When people live in a society, and these people have extra money to spend after they have taken care of their financial necessities, like bills and savings; they tend to recirculate money back into the general and local economy. This helps build the economy and reinforce prosperity by completing the necessary cycle. There is a reason money is called currency. Its true intention is to flow through our accounts and the economy like the currents of the ocean. This flow feeds the areas of our society that need nourishment. Currency only works when it is allowed to flow and move. When we stop it up in one place or another, it does no one any good.

While we are looking at the practical use of money, let's also take a look at money as an energetic tool. Money has its own Magick power. When you spend money, take specific note of your mindset and thoughts. Your feelings will communicate to the universe what you want more of. Whether you have a positive or negative mindset, you are telling the universe what you want. If your mindset is on bills and your resentment for them, you will attract more bills and resentment. If your mindset is on saving money and prosperity, you will have more money to save and prosperity.

It is for these reasons that I feel Magick should be used for our own personal gain. I am not saying you have to be ruthless and greedy. In fact, you get to choose what kind of prosperous Witch you will be. You can be generous and kind if you choose. Using Magick to take care of yourself is not about greed. The important point here is that you live a life where you are well cared for. You should have the money and means to pay your bills, care for your loved ones (including your fur babies) while having enough money to cycle back into your local economy. There is no reasonable shame in using Magick to help you accomplish this.

Now, let's take a look at using Magick on others. Within most Wiccan traditions using Magick on others without their specific knowledge or permission is taboo. Since I am not Wiccan, I don't necessarily follow this philosophy. Keep in mind that Magick doesn't have to be about changing or disrupting someone's personal will. Instead, it can be about atmosphere. Kitchen Witchery usually means you will infuse some sort of Magickal intent into just about every meal you create… whether you know it or not. If you love to cook the passion you have for food and cooking will always be there, and rightly so! You should cook with joy and conviction, and every meal you create will reflect this!

When I serve my meals to my family, they know my food is Magickally charged. They have no issue with eating the meals I create because they know I do not intend anything malicious with my workings. Many friends and family are eager to partake because of the feelings, and flavors they experience. They can feel my joy and love for cooking. They can feel my love of the ingredients I choose, as well as my thoroughness and devotion in their preparation. Meals are a positive experience, felt with every bite taken.

This still brings up the question of Magickal influences on personal will and performing Magick on others who are unaware. Some practitioners are very careful to not interfere with another's will or to cast spells on, or have others partake in spell work without specific consent. This can be a sticky issue for the Kitchen Witch. Just about everything you create will in some way contain influential power - your influential power. However, there is a modification you can practice if the ethics of spellcasting without specific permission is an issue.

A good example is when we have guests or when we are preparing foods for a potluck style gathering. Perhaps those who will consume the food you create are not familiar with your path. Let's face it not everyone needs to know your personal details. This is when I tend to refocus my workings. I make the atmosphere for the event my Magickal focus. The energy I put into my recipe will mostly influence me, and my demeanor. I will focus on creating good conversation, friendship, and comfort for my guests during the event. I focus on awakening my inner hostess and social butterfly, who will allow me to lighten social awkwardness.

Serving other's your Magickal recipes does not have to involve a serious debate on ethics. Turning your Magickal focus toward yourself is an ideal way to relieve the issue of using Magick on others. In any Magickal working, the key is to harness your own power and intensely focus your desires to move in the direction you need and want.

Cooking with Others

This is one of my most favorite things to do. I love to cook with others. I invite family and friends over anytime I get a chance. We host barbeques, garden tea parties, dinners and even desserts and drinks when we want to keep it simple. I invite everyone to help me chop, mince, mix and so on. The collaboration of cooking together becomes a socially Magickal experience.

Cooking together is a fabulous way to connect with one another. After all, much of any social and societal interaction involves food. We celebrate with food. We mourn with food. We talk over tea and coffee. Food is intertwined into the fabric of our culture, we simply can't go without it.

When you can invite others into your Magickal space and share with them your techniques and ideas, you strengthen bonds. This is a wonderful bonding element that can benefit Covens and Coven Mates on a social and spiritual level. Each person can take on a specific task and place their own personal energy into the meal aka spell work. Then, when it is all said and done, you all sit together to enjoy the results of your cooperative working.

I am a firm believer that all who claim ownership or participation in a coven should absolutely take part in every aspect and activity of the Coven. Covens are not church congregations where we sit on the sidelines to be preached at. Instead, our spiritual experiences are meant to be hands-on; Kitchen Witchery is a fabulous way to do this. I highly recommend getting your coven's butt in the kitchen and cook! The key is to give everyone an ingredient, have them prepare their ingredient while infusing it with the intended Magickal focus.

Cooking together as a Coven not only is great for spell work but also makes a great tradition for Sabbats and other rituals or observances. Think back to when you were a kid, and you baked cookies (or some other holiday recipe) for Thanksgiving or Christmas with your family. This is an excellent example of how groups of people, like covens, can come together to celebrate a Sabbat, ritual, or another special event. Together you essentially build upon and reinforce your traditions and values. As you do this, you create lasting and meaningful memories.

Ready for Magick?

There is more to Magick than candles and chants, it is something that stirs within you.

It is something that bubbles up to give you goosebumps.

Magick is that prickling sensation that lets you know, energy is moving in the right direction!

When you are ready to perform Magick using a recipe spell, you will want to create the right template that suits your needs. Soon, I will discuss finding the right recipe, but first, we should put together all the other aspects of spell work; in conjunction with the topics previously discussed. I didn't put the subjects of atmosphere, organization, the elements, etc. in this book to create fillers - No, they are critical to conducting, creating, and successfully manifesting your needs and desires.

When you have your space organized, and the atmosphere is just right, you will need to turn your attention to flow. Magickal flow. How will your spells be conducted? What comes first, second and last? You will want to create for yourself a template to help you move swiftly into the mindset of creating Magick.

Using a template will allow you to organize yourself quickly and will free your thoughts allowing you to focus more clearly on your intentions. Here is how I prefer to conduct my Magick in my kitchen. This will give you an idea of how you can make Kitchen Magick simple.

1. I make sure my kitchen is in order, going back to cleanliness and organization. Seriously, I wipe down the counters, sweep, mop, etc. If you are doing this often, you will only need a few minutes to declutter.

2. I decide on my goal. I make it very clear in my mind exactly what I need and want from my recipe and spell work.

3.   I choose my main ingredient(s) related to my goal. This helps determine the recipe I will create and helps me choose additional complimentary ingredients. Having a resource (like a quick reference chart) that quickly reminds me of what properties relate to which ingredient saves me time and frustration.

4.   I find a suitable recipe and gather my ingredients. This requires some planning and possibly shopping. Planning is essential in most Magickal actions, and more so when Magickal recipes are the medium.

5.   Adorn the Apron! I have several, so I choose the apron that best suits my energetic needs at the time. As I place my apron over my head and tie the string, I am transcended into a Magickal mindset.

6.   Organize the ingredients. I want to easily reach and identify what I need when I need it. This is where some prep and misen place comes in handy. If you have read over your recipe, you will know where to begin, and you can start chopping, dicing, and measuring your ingredients.

7.   Time to reinforce the right mindset. I light some candles, smolder some spices as incense, I breathe deep, and relax my mind so I can begin.

8.   Finally, I CREATE! It is time to focus completely on my Magick and recipe! This is where you want to really feel the energy of your intention. Be conscious of your ingredients, your thoughts, their purpose, etc. If you have a chant or mantra you feel is appropriate, repeat this as you create your recipe.

This breakdown might make the process seem complicated or daunting. Instead of hyper-focusing on each task, think about the whole process more practically. You do most of these things all the time, the only difference is that I laid them out for you; pointing out the details. Stay positive! You already do this work, some days you may even be able to do it in your sleep. This is easy stuff, and it only gets easier the more you do it.

Did you ever wonder why people are attracted to long, elaborate rituals, where there is music, scent, and beautiful things to look at? Rituals are templates, much like the one I have shared with you. They allow us to sink into the mindset of Spirituality, Magick, and wonder more easily. When we create our own ritual templates, we will find ourselves dropping into the right mindset quickly for Magickal and spiritual purposes. Think about all the things that help you feel spiritual, relaxed, and connected to Divinity. Use what speaks to you and follow a template that allows you to connect more completely with your higher self.

Stirring the "Pot."

Many Kitchen Witches stir their foods in a very specific way. Call me a rebel, but I do not necessarily follow this model. Most Kitchen Witches I know will only stir in a clockwise or a deosil motion. I prefer to go with my gut on this one. Magick is not one-sided, so unless the direction in which you stir weighs heavily on the result of your Magickal working, I would not stress this too much. Directional focus matters most often when you are seeking to attract and/or repel specific energy. If you are focusing on banishing energy as you stir, then you should stir in a widdershins, or counterclockwise motion. If you are focused on attracting energies, then you should stir in a clockwise or deosil motion. It is possible that within one recipe or working you can have a need to stir in both directions, it's completely up to you. Directional stirring is not something I get stirred up about.

Recipes

Yes, I did say this was not a cookbook. However, I have included a few recipes that will help get you started. I want to give you a good feel for how you can create your own Magick in the Kitchen. The following recipes will outline for you how each ingredient plays its own role in representing your Magickal intentions.

The recipes I have selected range in need, desire, and intent. Each recipe includes notes about the specific ingredients and how to use them. This will give you a better sense of how you can create your own recipes, and how you can incorporate Magickal intent into existing recipes.

The recipes to follow are some of my favorites and are not available on my blog. You have first and exclusive access to these delicious Magickal Creations.

ENJOY!!!

Communication Salad

This recipe is intended to influence positive communication between you, and someone you need to speak with regarding a serious or potentially volatile subject. This is also a great spell to perform before you need to give a speech.

Ingredients:

Finely shredded zest of 2 lemons

1/4 cup Extra Virgin olive oil

1/4 cup fresh lemon juice

1/2 teaspoon sugar

10 ounces cooked great northern beans, drained and rinsed

15 ounces cooked chickpeas, drained and rinsed

Ice water

10-ounces green beans, trimmed and cut into 1" pieces

6 green onions thinly sliced diagonally

½ Stalk celery sliced thin

Salt and Pepper to taste

Instructions:

1. In a small bowl, whisk together lemon zest, lemon juice, sugar, and salt; drizzle in the oil as you whisk. Set aside.

2. Use a steamer or a large saucepan with simmering water; steam-blanch the green beans, for 4 to 5 minutes. Shock the green beans with ice water, then drain and pat dry with a kitchen towel.

3. In a large serving bowl combine all the ingredients minus the ice water, and top with dressing and toss to coat. Season with salt and pepper to taste.

4. Chill in the refrigerator for 2-3 hours or up to 1 day. Serve cold.

Communication Salad, Ingredient Attributes & Spell Work Notes

This spell does not have to be consumed by anyone other than you. As you prep and mix all of your ingredients, you will need to have a clear and determined focus on your intent for this spell. Below is a breakdown that will help queue your intentional focus during the process of preparing your ingredients and mixing the salad.

Onion: Removing Obstacles – This ingredient's job is to help you remove mental obstacles, blocks, and hurdles that prevent you from speaking clearly. While you slice the onions, you should be focused on speaking clearly as you use the tone and words that are appropriate for the situation.

Celery: Mental Powers – Not to be confused with physic powers. This ingredient's job is to help you focus clearly on what needs to be said. It will help you maintain mental focus and clarity as you relay your concerns, organize your thoughts, and express your viewpoints in the conversation. As you slice the celery focus on your target points related to the subject(s) of your conversation.

Lemon: Happiness & Friendship - Because good communication happens best when we are feeling happy and friendly, lemon is a critical ingredient in this recipe. When you zest, slice, and juice the lemon focus on happiness, and friendship with the participants of the conversation. This focus should be continued as you whisk your lemon with your other dressing ingredients.

Beans: Reconciliation- If your need for this spell does not require reconciliation, then you can leave this part out. This is mainly for conversations that require you and the opposing party to come to a truce or agreement. This ingredient can also help you reconcile your own inner issues related to the subject to be discussed. Use this Magickal focus at your discretion. As you prepare the beans, focus on reconciling differences, resolving anger, dissolving fears, and reaching agreements.

Grilled Creativity Chicken Salad

This is a great salad for those who seek and participate in creative endeavors. If you are looking to create something to sell or display, this is the recipe for you. This spell is about strengthening your creative flow as well as your mental ability to create. As I mentioned before the reason, I do not box foods, herbs, and spices into too few categories is because in many cases, one food can serve multiple purposes. This salad displays the versatility of Magickal Ingredients very clearly.

Ingredients:

3 cups boneless skinless grill chicken breasts, sliced

2 tablespoons extra-virgin olive oil

3 tablespoons fresh lime juice

1 tablespoon chili powder

1 teaspoon cumin, ground

3 cups packed mixed greens with kale

1 cup jicama, chopped

2 avocados, halved, pitted and cubed

1 red bell pepper, chopped

1/4 cup cilantro leaves

2 scallions, sliced

Cherry tomatoes

Salt & Pepper to taste

Shredded Parmesan cheese (optional)

Instructions:

In a large mixing bowl, add cumin, chili powder & lime juice. As you whisk together these ingredients and slowly drizzle in the oil. Add chicken and toss to coat. Salt and pepper to taste.

On a platter or in a serving bowl layer the remaining ingredients as follows: salad greens, cilantro, and scallions. Top with red bell pepper, jicama, chicken, tomatoes, and avocado and serve immediately. Drizzle with dressing and serve.

Grilled Creativity Chicken Salad, Ingredient Attributes & Spell Work Notes

Consuming this salad before you create is ideal. The ingredients complement one another helping you boost creativity, sell your work, and protect against harm. If you are a writer, an artist, or a professional crafter should make this salad often. If you can create this recipe and spell work during the full moon on a Wednesday, your chance of success and potency will be optimized.

Jicama: Creativity - Promotes the sale of your work. Especially, when eaten during the full moon.

Cilantro: Mental Strength, Awareness, Creativity & Attracts Money for creative endeavors - Eat Cilantro on Wednesday to boost your creativity.

Kale: Beating out the competition - This will help your work shine brighter than the rest, making your pieces more attractive to potential buyers.

Cumin: Protection - We all need a little protection from negative energies that come our way, and let's face it in the art & craft market there is plenty to go around. Cumin is known to protect against theft. This unique spice can play a large role in deterring others from "copying," and stealing your work.

Employment Breakfast Parfait .

This is a great spell for securing employment, maintaining employment, or getting a promotion. You should perform this spell on the morning of your interview or as often as you see necessary.

Ingredients:

6-ounces plain yogurt

3 medium strawberries, cut into pieces

1-ounce chopped pecans

Honey to drizzle

Cinnamon to taste

Instructions:

In a clear glass cup or Parfait glass, layer the yogurt and then strawberries. Drizzle with a little honey and top with the pecans and cinnamon.

Employment Breakfast Parfait, Ingredient Attributes & Spell Work Notes

When you slice your berries and layer your parfait, imagine yourself in the interview overflowing with confidence, knowledge, and strength. As each layer rises, envision yourself rising to the top, surpassing your competition. If you are performing this spell before you submit your resume, envision your resume being placed at the top of every resume pile. Envision your experience, knowledge, and skills being exactly what the potential employer needs and wants.

Also, brew and drink coffee with this recipe to add further benefit and strength to your working.

Yogurt: Employment – Yogurt, like milk, is often used in conjunction with Honey as a libation and for spell work associated with prosperity. Use yogurt any time to boost your chances of job manifestation and retention.

Strawberries: Luck – When you are finished enjoying your sweet and delicious strawberries you can carry strawberry leaves in your pocket for an added boost of luck.

Pecans: Employment – If you can buy pecans unshelled, you can perform a visualization of you working and enjoying your job as you slowly de-shell each pecan. Otherwise, this visualization can be done as you chew.

Honey: Good Fortune – Honey has long been associated with prosperity, money, and good fortune. Solidify the potency of your spell by envisioning your success as you drizzle honey into your parfait.

Cinnamon: Success – Fiery cinnamon always brings a boost of success and motivation to spell work. When adding cinnamon to your Magickal recipe be sure to inhale its aroma and feel it uplift and motivate you to succeed.

Peach-Rosemary Jam

Together Peach and Rosemary create a powerful protective team. This jam uses less sugar and no pectin allowing the flavor of the peaches and rosemary to shine. My family thought I was nuts mixing these flavors together until they tried it. Now it is the favorite jam of my household.

Ingredients

4 pounds of fresh Peaches (about 16 peaches)

3 cups of Sugar

2 Tablespoons of Lemon Juice

1/2 cup of Water

2 Sprigs of Rosemary

Instructions

Canning Prep:

Wash jars and bands in hot, soapy water. Rinse

Place jars in a canner filled with water, bring to boil.

Boil jars for 15 minutes to sterilize.

Place lids and bands in warm water, do not boil. Leave until ready to use.

Peach Jam Recipe:

Rinse the peaches under cool running water.

Place whole fresh peaches in a pot of boiling water for 60 seconds or until the peel begins to recede.

Remove from the boiling water and place in ice water to stop the cooking process.

Peel peaches, remove the pit, slice each quarter into 2 or 3 chunks. (This is the messy part. You might want to wear an apron)

Place cut peaches in a food processor, add lemon juice and pulse into small bits careful not to liquefy.

Place a pot on the stove, set to medium heat.

Add water, then sugar; bring to a gentle boil and stir until sugar is dissolved. About 2 minutes.

Add peach pulp, stir and simmer over medium heat until mixture becomes thick. This will take several minutes up to an hour.

Stir frequently to prevent burning.

In the last 30 minutes of cooking add your rosemary sprigs. Remove spring before ladling into prepared jars.

When done, ladle into hot jars, leaving 1/4 inch headspace.

Remove air bubbles, wipe rim, place lid & band then tighten.

Process 10 minutes in a boiling water bath canner or according to your altitude.

Remove and cool for 24 hours in a cool location. On the counter at room temperature is good.

Store your jam in a cool dark place for a year or longer.

Recipe Notes:

Canning is very easy, don't over think it. If you are a beginner, there are plenty of resources available teaching you the basics of how to can and preserve food. While it is fairly easy, the process is time-consuming and requires a little knowledge for success. You should have basic cooking knowledge, the right tools, and an understanding of the canning process before you begin.

The benefits of canning and preserving your own food is unmistakable. Not only will you save money, but you will also be able to enjoy the taste of summer all year long. One of my favorite things to do with my jams and preserves is to give them away as delicious holiday gifts!

Peach-Rosemary Jam, Ingredient Attributes & Spell Work Notes

Peach: Protection & Longevity – Once you have prepared your jam you can use the peach pits in your home for added benefit. Peach pits can be placed in window sills and above doorways to protect your home from unwanted intruders and energetic influences.

Rosemary: Protection & Healing - Not only can you use rosemary in recipes you can also add it to bath water and smolder as incense.

Esbat Cookies

Full Moon rituals are some of the most beloved among Witches and Pagans, alike. I enjoy making these cookies for both dark moon and full moon rituals. They are a tasty treat when you bask in the moon's gentle light.

Ingredients:

½ cup (1 stick) unsalted butter, cold, cut into cubes

1 tablespoon light cooking oil

½ cup granulated sugar

1 teaspoon vanilla extract

½ teaspoon Kosher Salt

1 large egg

¼ cup cornstarch

½ cup unsweetened dark cocoa powder

1¼- 1¾ cups all-purpose flour

White Royal Icing

Instructions:

Cream together the butter, oil, sugar, vanilla, and salt in the bowl of a stand mixer fitted with a paddle attachment, just until the mixture is smooth. Be careful to not overbeat.

Add the egg and mix until just incorporated.

Slowly incorporate the cornstarch, cocoa powder, and flour. Chill dough for about 2 hours.

Preheat the oven to 375° F.

Roll the dough out to ¼ inch thickness. Use a circle cookie cutter to make circle shaped cookies.

Bake circles on parchment-lined baking sheets for 9 to 12 minutes, depending on your oven and the size of your cookies. The cookie should look dry on the surface and be firm around the edges while remaining soft in the middle.

Cool completely before decorating.

To celebrate a full moon, cover the surface of your dark cookies with white icing. If you would like to use these cookies for a dark moon ritual, leave them plain.

Deviled Sabbat Eggs Recipe

Since each Sabbat has its specific food association, I found it hard to have one general recipe that can be served on any occasion. I always like to have that one recipe that can be adapted and modified to suit any celebration. This seems to be the most versatile recipe, and it is easy to create.

In the summer, this recipe can be lightened up with sour cream, and in the winter, it can be made with more traditional methods. In the spring and fall, you can add fresh herbs and spice. There are so many options and so few ways to go wrong. Here is my own Basic Devil Egg recipe you can alter for your next Sabbat celebration.

Ingredients:

6 hard-boiled or steamed eggs, peeled and halved

1/4 cup Mayonnaise

1 tsp. Dijon Mustard

1/2 tsp. white vinegar

Salt and Pepper to taste

Instructions:

Separate egg yolks from egg whites.

Mash egg yolks in small bowl. Stir in remaining ingredients except for the egg white halves.

Spoon or pipe yolk filling into egg whites. Chill, until ready to serve.

Try adding minced shallot, chives, dill and other herbs to the recipe. Another favorite is adding some spice like cayenne pepper. This is a versatile dish that can be molded to suit just about any need and celebration.

Conclusion

Thank you so much for reading Magick in the Kitchen. I hope you enjoyed this book and look forward to the books I will write in the future.

While I feel like I could speak in more detail about Kitchen Witchcraft, the spirituality of food, and the life of a Kitchen Witch, I also know that it is now your time to get cooking as you discover your own path in the Kitchen.

It has been my pleasure to share some of what I know, my rituals, and life with you. Perhaps someday we will meet in person, and we have a chance to discuss your path and the Magick it has brought you.

Brightest Blessings,

Leandra

www.TheMagickKitchen.com

www.LeandraWitchwood.com

About the Author

"I just want good food and to live a Magickal life!"

Is that so much to ask?

I believe it isn't, and through persistence, I found that I can have both!

I realize that I could forge my own path using the skills and knowledge I gained while harnessing a few simple techniques.

I love food and everything that goes with it. I have spent more than 40 years in the kitchen. Also, I have over 25 years studying various aspects of Wicca, Witchcraft, and Paganism. Combining these two interests has created a Magickal path where food and spirituality are the focus. To my delight, they play brilliantly together.

My love of healthy whole foods and unique recipes has also led me to help run a local teen cooking program, where I teach kids valuable life skills in the kitchen. I teach a variety of cooking classes for adults and covens on subjects ranging from making the time spent in the kitchen more enjoyable, to cooking together as a group, and Magickal recipe creation.

It only made sense that I would begin writing about and sharing my knowledge and experiences with the Witchcraft and Pagan communities. From this, The Magick Kitchen (www.TheMagickKitchen.com) was born.

My journey with you is about developing your spiritual relationship with food, far beyond the dull habit of consumption. We have a marvelous opportunity here to take something mundane and make it Magickal!

My personal journey is about connecting to Divinity through food and using the ritual of preparing and sharing food to create Magick! It is about developing a sacred balance between nourishment, ritual, and spirit. Food, herbs, spices, and Magickal recipes have the power to heal, change lives, and bring us together as friends, families, and community. It is my pleasure to help you work more closely with food in your spiritual practice as we develop your connected relationship through the seemingly mundane act of cooking.

Thank you for joining me!

Brightest Blessings!

Leandra Witchwood

www.LeandraWitchwood.com

www.TheMagickKitchen.com

Want MORE?
Discover more books by Leandra.

Available on Amazon!

Resources

Find me on social media and the web!

www.TheMagickKitchen.com

www.LeandraWitchwood.com

https://www.facebook.com/groups/WitchcraftEssentials/

https://www.instagram.com/leandrawitchwood/

Get ideas and connect with others through Confessions of Crafty Witches on Facebook

Find groups and events in your area: www.witchvox.com

Help support earth-center faiths: www.SpiritFire.org

Find Pagan Pride Festivals in your area: www.paganpride.org

Made in the USA
Middletown, DE
17 June 2020